Technological Innovation in American Local Governments
(PPS-17)

Pergamon Titles of Related Interest

Foster *Comparative Public Policy and Citizen Participation: Energy, Education, Health and Local Governance in the USA and Germany*

Hadley *The American Split Ticket Vote: Regional Realignment, Dealignment, or Status Quo?*

Savitch *Urban Policy and the Exterior City: Federal, State and Corporate Policies*

PERGAMON
POLICY
STUDIES

Technological Innovation in American Local Governments/The Case of Computing

James L. Perry
Kenneth L. Kraemer

Published in cooperation with the
Public Policy Research Organization,
University of California, Irvine

Pergamon Press

NEW YORK • OXFORD • TORONTO • SYDNEY • FRANKFURT • PARIS

52977

Pergamon Press Offices:

U.S.A.   Pergamon Press Inc., Maxwell House, Fairview Park,
                     Elmsford, New York 10523, U.S.A.

U.K.   Pergamon Press Ltd., Headington Hill Hall,
                     Oxford OX3 0BW, England

CANADA   Pergamon of Canada, Ltd., 150 Consumers Road,
                     Willowdale, Ontario M2J, 1P9, Canada

AUSTRALIA   Pergamon Press (Aust) Pty. Ltd., P O Box 544,
                     Potts Point, NSW 2011, Australia

FRANCE   Pergamon Press SARL, 24 rue des Ecoles,
                     75240 Paris, Cedex 05, France

FEDERAL REPUBLIC Pergamon Press GmbH, 6242 Kronberg/Taunus,
OF GERMANY   Pferdstrasse 1, Federal Republic of Germany

Library of Congress Cataloging in Publication Data

Perry, James L
    Technological innovation in American local governments.

    (Pergamon policy studies)
    Bibliography: p.
    Includes index.
    1. Local government—United States—Data processing.
I. Kraemer, Kenneth L., joint author. II. Title.
JS344.E4P47   1979   352.16'0973   78-26458
ISBN 0-08-023707-X

This book is based upon research supported by the National Science
Foundation, Division of Policy Research and Analysis under Grant No.
PRA 76-15549. The views and conclusions contained in this report
are those of the authors and do not reflect the official position
of the National Science Foundation.

Printed in the United States of America

This book is dedicated to
Wendy Perry and Norine Kraemer
whose patience and support
have sustained us.

Contents

LIST OF FIGURES   ix

LIST OF TABLES   xi

ACKNOWLEDGMENTS   xiii

INTRODUCTION   1

PART I.   DIFFUSION OF COMPUTER APPLICATIONS
               AMONG LOCAL GOVERNMENTS   15

CHAPTER

    1   THE INFLUENCE OF INNOVATION ATTRIBUTES
               AND POLICY INTERVENTIONS   17

    2   THE INFLUENCE OF COOPERATION IN URBAN
               INTERGOVERNMENTAL NETWORKS ON
               DIFFUSION, TRANSFER, AND RESOURCE
               SHARING   39

    3   THE INFLUENCE OF MARKET VARIABLES   52

PART II.   ADOPTION OF COMPUTER APPLICATIONS BY
               LOCAL GOVERNMENTS   71

    4   ENVIRONMENTAL DETERMINANTS   73

    5   STAFFING AND ORGANIZATIONAL
               INFLUENCES   91

6   DETERMINANTS OF CHIEF EXECUTIVE
             SUPPORT   103

PART III.   RESEARCH FINDINGS   117

7   ASSESSMENT OF DIFFUSION AND ADOPTION   119

8   ASSESSMENT OF FEDERAL POLICY   126

APPENDIX 1. DATA SOURCES   137

APPENDIX 2. OPERATIONAL DEFINITIONS OF THE VARIABLES
             EMPLOYED IN THE ANALYSES   141

NOTES   153

REFERENCES   161

INDEX   169

ABOUT THE AUTHORS   173

List of Figures

Figure   Page

1   Cumulative Percentage of U.S. Cities and Counties
         Utilizing Computers, Based upon only those Govern-
         ments indicating Year of Adoption, Over all Respond-
         ing Governments, N=1063 Cities and 400 Counties   4

2   Patterns of Computer Application Development in
         Local Governments, by Major Subsystems   6

3   Related Dimensions of Federal Policy for Computer
         Technology Transfer   8

4   An Analytic Model of Technological Innovation in
         Local Government   12

5   Expansion of the Systems Characteristics Compo-
         nent of the Analytic Model   21

6   Expansion of the Subsystems Characteristics
         Component of the Analytic Model   43

7   Expansion of the Market Characteristics Component
         of the Analytic Model   55

8   Expansion of the Local Government Environment
         Component of the Conceptual Model   75

9   Hypothesized Relationships between the Four Con-
         ceptual Dimensions and Adoptability   79

10   Operational Relationships between the Four Conceptual
         Dimensions and Adoptability   81

Figure   Page

11   Operational Relationships between Adoptability and
            the Individual Components of Integration (I), Risk (R),
            and Need (N)   82

12   Expansion of the Staffing and Organizational Arrange-
            ments Components of the Analytic Model   94

13   Path Model for Innovation Magnitude Showing Significant
            Paths Among the Study Variables   97

14   Path Model for Innovation Scope Showing Significant
            Paths Among the Study Variables   98

15   Expansion of the Executive Support Component of
            the Analytic Model   106

16   Alternative Models of the Relationships Among
            Development Status, the Technology-Related
            Indicators and Current Utility   113

17   Related Dimensions of Federal Policy for
            Computer Technology Transfer   130

List of Tables

Table		Page
1	Computer Application Diffusion Patterns Among Local Governments	24
2	Expected Relationships between the Innovation Attributes, Policy Interventions, and Extent and Rate of Adoption of Computer Applications	27
3	Multiple Linear Regressions for Extent and Rate of Computer Application Adoption	29
4	Discriminant Functions for the Innovation Attributes and Policy Interventions	32
5	Diffusion Group Membership of the Computer Applications Predicted by the Discriminant Functions for the Six Group Criterion	33
6	Computer Applications Included in the Diffusion Groups	34
7	Expected Relationships between Diffusion, Transfer, and Resource Sharing and the Independent Variables	46
8	Zero-order Correlations Between the Independent Variables and Diffusion, Transfer and Resource Sharing	48
9	Multiple Regression Results for Rate of Diffusion, Transfer and Resource Sharing in Urban Intergovernmental Networks	49
10	Extensiveness of Application Transfer Among Surveyed Local Governments	57

Table		Page
11	Plans for Computer Applications Transfer Among Surveyed Local Governments	58
12	Overlap of Local Governments That Have Transferred and Plan to Transfer Computer Applications	59
13	A Breakdown of Local Governments Transferring Computer Applications, by Population	60
14	Comparative Technical Sophistication Among Local Governments That Have Transferred Applications	61
15	Similarity and Proximity of Transfer Sites (N=113)	62
16	Source of Transferred Applications	62
17	Technical Compatibility of Host Computers of Transferred Applications	63
18	Sophistication of Applications Transferred	64
19	Illustrative Applications Transferred	65
20	Factor Loadings and Definitions for the Domain, Integration, and Risk Variables	78
21	Multiple Linear Regressions for the Components of Each Conceptual Dimension and Adoption	85
22	R^2's for Three of the Dimensions when Stratified by Scores of the Fourth Dimension	86
23	Summary of Propositions Relating Executive Support to Innovation in Government Organizations	93
24	Items Used in Developing the Current and Expected Utility Scales	107
25	Expectations about the Relationships between the Independent Variables and the Current and Expected Utility Scales	110
26	Zero-order Correlations between the Antecedent Variables and the Current and Expected Utility Scales	111
27	Multiple Regression Results for the Independent Variables and the Current and Expected Utility Scales	114

Acknowledgments

We wish to express our thanks to the many individuals who contributed to the preparation of this book. J. David Roessner, of the National Science Foundation, provided critical comments at various stages between formulation of the research objectives and completion of the research upon which this book is based. We also wish to express our appreciation to the many colleagues from UCI and other universities who contributed helpful comments and suggestions. Bill Dutton, Les Berkes, George Downs, Robert Eyestone, Irwin Feller, John Leslie King, Rob Kling, Charles Levine, Joe Matthews, Lyman Porter, and Kenneth Warner shared their views with us. Jim Danziger contributed in an even more direct way by co-authoring Chapter 4.

Many other individuals had a hand in the creation of the book. Mark Pittel, our research assistant, efficiently and accurately carried out the varied tasks we called upon him to perform. Sig Fidyke served equally well as our interface with the computer for the hundreds of statistical analyses we performed. Deborah Silverman not only edited the book manuscript, but also assisted the authors in substantive decisions about format, content and style. The Public Policy Research Organization (PPRO) administrative staff, Dave Schetter, Shirley Hoberman, and Doris McBride, contributed their skills to assure the smooth management of the budgetary, reporting and office supervisory side of the project. Helen Sandoz painstakingly prepared the tables and figures. Finally, we thank the PPRO secretarial staff, Nan Brock, Helen Sandoz, Georgine Webster, and Betty Kelly, for their care and patience in preparing the many drafts of this book.

To acknowledge the contributions of two people whose support has literally been continuous, we dedicate this book to our wives, Wendy and Norine.

Introduction

In introducing the analyses in this book, this chapter provides the reader with requisite characteristics of computer applications which make them particularly fruitful sources of data on innovation, and the government activity and policy contexts in which they are used are described. An explanation of the theoretical approach taken in the analyses, and brief descriptions of the specific topics covered are then presented.

Increasing efficiency and productivity in the civilian sectors of the economy through innovation is a continuing national concern. By exploring the structures and decisions underlying innovation diffusion and adoption, we seek to identify variables that influence innovation and to provide a basis for understanding the effects of public and private involvement. Through these efforts, we aim to develop a better understanding of the interrelated activities that produce technological innovations and that lead to their application and, thus, to enable policymakers to improve the timeliness, extent, and effectiveness of their interventions.(1)

In addressing these general issues, this book brings research to bear on the effects of policy interventions on a particular class of technological innovations − computers − and a particular class of organizational units − local governments. To clarify the significance of this perspective, and its relationship to the larger areas with which we are concerned, we will present first some general background information about computers and their use in local government activities, and some characteristics of federal policy toward the diffusion of computer applications.

1

COMPUTER APPLICATIONS AS INNOVATIONS

As a multi-use, multidimensional technology, computing is an unusually fruitful source of data on innovation. Computerized systems are the focal technologies of this study, but are analyzed within a large body of knowledge concerning technological innovations in general, and innovations in local governments in particular.

For the purposes of analysis, computing represents a complex technological "package" which encompasses an interdependent system composed of people (users, computer specialists, managers), apparatus (including hardware such as computer mainframes and peripherals, software such as operating systems and applications programs, and data) and techniques (procedures, practices, organizational arrangements) necessary to use the apparatus within the context of local government (The URBIS Group, in process; Illich, 1973). The study of computing as a technical innovation generally involves a focus on either the technological apparatus – computer hardware and associated software – or computer applications.

We focus on the diffusion of computer applications among American local governments rather than the diffusion of computers themselves. We have made this distinction not only because federal policy interventions are typically aimed at applications rather than computers per se, but also because of the greater potential that applications hold for the understanding of diffusion processes. While the initial decision to adopt a computer is important, it is significantly different from the richer, more complex, and continuous streams of decisions which are involved in the adoption of computer applications. First, a decision whether or not to adopt a computer is fairly straightforward; but the application adoption process involves an explicit "life cycle" of decisions including initiation, development or transfer, operation, and, eventually, redevelopment or discontinuation. Second, computer adoption decisions involve large investments which seldom are discontinued; whereas application adoption decisions involve incremental investments which might be altered substantially at any of several stages in the adoption process.

COMPUTING IN LOCAL GOVERNMENT

Magnitude of Computing

The local government sector is considered an area for major payoffs from technological innovations aimed at improving productivity because of its increasing demand for services in the face of a declining base of resources (Miller, 1977; National Commission on Productivity, 1971). Since the local government sector is highly labor intensive, it is hoped that significant productivity improvements can be achieved by replacing labor with capital investments in technology (Roessner, forthcoming; 1976). Nowhere is this more apparent than in the diffusion of computer technology among local governments.

Indeed, computer technology has become a common element of the day-to-day operations of government at all levels since its introduction in the early 1950s. Recent surveys of computing in local governments indicate that virtually every city and county with populations over 50,000 and about half of the governments with populations between 10,000 and 50,000 utilize computers in some facet of their operations (Kraemer, et al., 1978). It is interesting to note that the pattern of computer adoptions has tended to follow the traditional S-shaped curve for diffusion of other technical innovations (Fig. 1). This overall pattern suggests that smaller governments will continue to adopt computers until most have adopted them sometime within the next decade.

The significance of computer technology in local governments is illustrated by the magnitude of total expenditures for computing. A recent Nation's Cities report (Kraemer, et al., 1975b: 18) reveals:

Local governments currently spend over $1 billion annually on EDP, and this figure will double within a decade. The federal government has been intensively involved in local government EDP, spending up to $200 million per year and supporting research, development, pilot programs and operations on a variety of local information systems.

These aggregate local government outlays translate to each local government currently spending about two to three percent of its operating budget on computing.

Magnitude of Computer Application Adoption

The city and county government surveys also indicate that potentially there are 300 different generic computer applications in 27 different government functions. Currently, city and county governments with populations of more than 10,000 report an average of about 19 different automated activities, with a range from four applications automated on the average for the smallest governments to 50 applications automated on the average for the largest governments. Accounting, revenue collection, and utilities applications dominate the current set of uses in local governments, with more than half of recently surveyed governments reporting such uses. Other major uses include police protection, assessment, budget and management, purchasing and inventory and personnel (Kraemer, et al., 1975a).

The current sophistication of computer applications varies widely in local governments. Kraemer, et al. (1975a) identify six categories of computer applications and report the percent of use in each category for all cities and counties surveyed as:

1) Record Keeping   42%

2) Calculating/Printing   35%

3) Record Searching   8%

4) Record Restructuring   6%

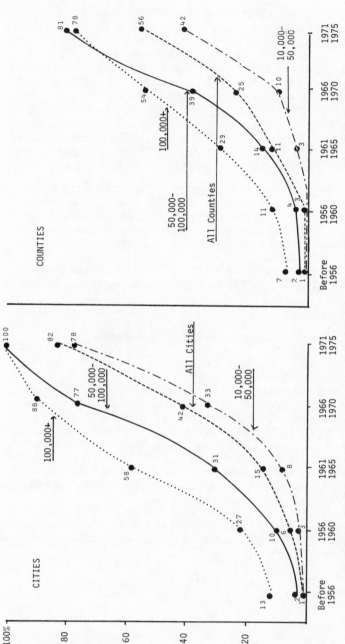

Figure 1. CUMULATIVE PERCENTAGE OF U.S. CITIES AND COUNTIES UTILIZING COMPUTERS, BASED UPON ONLY THOSE GOVERNMENTS INDICATING YEAR OF ADOPTION, OVER ALL RESPONDING GOVERNMENTS, N=1063 CITIES AND 400 COUNTIES[a]

[a]This estimate is based upon only those governments that responded and does not include those that were automated but did not answer. For cities over 50,000 and counties over 100,000, the number of governments using computers is based upon only cities and counties having in-house computers; cities and counties with service bureaus, regional installations or outside sources were not included. For the smaller cities and counties all sources of computing were included. Thus, the estimates tend to be low for the larger cities and counties and high for the smaller governments. The data for this figure is from a 1975 ICMA survey of cities between 10,000 and 50,000 in population and counties between 10,000 and 100,000 in population, and from the URBIS survey of the larger cities and counties (Appendix 1).

5) Sophisticated Analytics   5%

6) Process Control   3%

These categories vary on a continuum from relatively simple tasks to more complex simulation and control tasks, and serve to illustrate the wide qualitative diversity of computer applications in use.

In the future, applications of the computer are expected to increase in terms of the breadth of local government functions automated, the number of applications used in specific government functions, and the sophistication of applications adopted. Areas in which computer applications are expected to grow include finance, police and fire protection, courts, planning and zoning (Kraemer, et al., 1975a).

FEDERAL POLICY TOWARDS COMPUTING
IN AMERICAN LOCAL GOVERNMENTS

Significance of Computing in the Federal System

Clearly, the magnitude of past and future computer adoption in local governments demands investigation to assure that resources are being obtained and employed effectively. However, as we noted previously, federal and state policy towards local government computing is rarely directed at computer adoption per se. Rather, it is directed most often at the development or transfer of computer applications. Thus, understanding the processes by which computer applications are introduced to particular government units and the processes involved in widespread diffusion of particular applications is especially relevant to our examination of federal and state policy interventions. To the extent that these processes are thoroughly understood, informed decisions can be made regarding federal policy towards support for the diffusion of specific applications and for the development of computing generally within local governments.

The Extent of Federal Involvement

Federal involvement in local computing, as measured by investment, is substantial; about $250 million in assistance is provided annually to state and local governments (Davis, 1972). This federal investment, however, represents less than 25 percent of the total investment in local computing. Local governments themselves spend approximately $1 billion annually. Since the greatest proportion of the investment is made by the local governments, local computing is strongly shaped by local objectives.

The current pattern of automation in local governments reflects primary concern with revenue maintenance objectives(2) in the area of public finance and administration (Fig. 2). In recent years, automation has also increased in the area of public safety, partly as a result of direct federal financial assistance to cities for law enforcement automation beginning around 1968.(3) In contrast, community development and public works, human resources, and general government functions have proceeded at a relatively low level of automation despite substantial federal assistance in the area of human resources and sporadic assistance in the area of community development and public works (Fig. 2).(4)

Federal investment in local government computing generally has been applied at the margins of existing development and has been aimed at incremental improvements designed to serve primarily federal objectives. The impact of these interventions has been varied. This is partially because of the tension that exists between federal and local objectives, and partially because of differences in the effectiveness of the design approaches and transfer mechanisms used to achieve these objectives. Each of these dimensions of federal policy — <u>objectives, design approaches, transfer mechanisms</u> — is

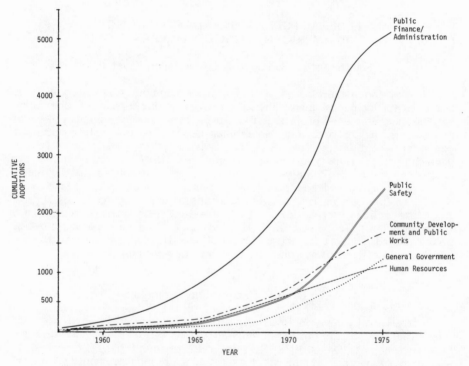

Figure 2.   PATTERNS OF COMPUTER APPLICATION DEVELOPMENT IN LOCAL GOVERNMENTS, BY MAJOR SUBSYSTEMS

illustrated in Fig. 3 and elaborated upon next.

Duality of Federal Objectives for Involvement

Federal assistance has served both local and federal needs.(5) Some federal efforts have attempted to fill gaps in the local application market. These gaps existed because local government operations in many service areas had no analogues in the private sector. Unlike many core organizational functions such as accounting and budgeting, applications for police, fire and social services lacked a strong "market pull" from the private sector. Thus, they were less likely to be available from vendors. Federal support also was provided to extend the use of automation from routine operations to urban planning and management. Support for planning was focused on transportation and land use planning, economic development, housing, and urban renewal in the form of urban databanks and urban development models. Support for management was limited and ad hoc.

While local objectives have been served by federal policy, the motivations for federal support of local government computing have originated more from federal than from local objectives. The increasing federal involvement in local activities during the 1960s led to support of computer applications for the collection of local data on housing, employment and education needed by federal agencies. The statistics derived from local data could be used to demonstrate the need for federal programs, to evaluate requests by local agencies for federal assistance, and to evaluate federal programs on a continuing basis. Computing also opened attractive opportunities for the support of applications which would improve local ability to cope with critical problems and thereby enhance the effectiveness of federal programs. Thus, computerized information and referral systems become part of the federal strategy of "social services integration"; automated wants/warrants and prosecution management information systems become part of the "war on crime," and urban databanks become part of "model cities."

These federal objectives represent both a strictly federal interest in nationwide statistics and an enlightened federal interest in the local problems of an increasingly urban society. While these objectives are compatible in theory, they often have been incompatible in practice (Rogers, Eveland & Klepper, 1977). Spending federal monies for strictly federal purposes has generally been considered appropriate, but spending federal monies for essentially local purposes has been controversial. As a result, automation in support of statistics gathering has been stable and funded at an increasing level, whereas automation in support of expanded local application of computer technology has been unstable and characterized by periods of both feast and famine.

Design Approaches for Computer Applications

Software design has a significant bearing on the implementation of federal objectives because of problems which may arise around design performance, design economy, the manufacturability of the software, the size of the

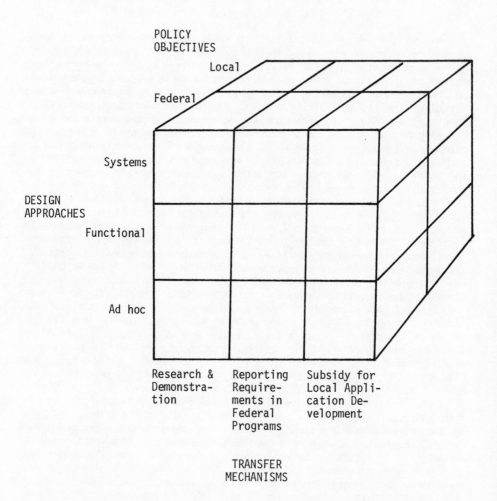

Figure 3.   RELATED DIMENSIONS OF FEDERAL POLICY FOR
COMPUTER TECHNOLOGY TRANSFER

potential market, and the performance expectations of end-users (House, Jones, & Bevilacqua, 1977). Federal approaches to the design of computer applications software can be characterized as: systems, functional, and ad hoc.

The systems approach is the software design equivalent of rational-comprehensive policymaking (Lindblom, 1959). The work of the federal Urban Information Systems Inter-Agency Committee (USAC) is a prime example of an implementation of this approach (Government Data Systems, 1971; Kraemer, 1971; Nation's Cities, 1972). To accomplish its general charge – the enhancement of urban information systems through intergovernmental cooperation – USAC aimed to develop data bases from local jurisdictions which would serve intergovernmental data requirements and facilitate integrated local planning and execution of discrete federal programs. The research conducted by USAC suggested that the primary means of achieving this end was to build "comprehensive" and "integrated" information systems in local governments as "building blocks" for intergovernmental systems. This comprehensive approach was expected to provide local spillovers which would more than justify the local participation and investment required.

The functional approach to applications software design involves the development of a range of applications for a local government operating agency by its federal counterpart. Perhaps the best examples of the use of the functional approach are the geoprocessing applications for local planning agencies developed by the Census Bureau and the criminal justice applications for local police agencies developed by the Law Enforcement Assistance Administration (LEAA).

The ad hoc approach, with its temporary involvement of federal agencies, most frequently has produced stand-alone, narrow-purpose software designs. Examples include the community shelter planning applications of the Office of Civil Defense and the fire service applications of the Departments of Commerce and Housing and Urban Development.

Federal Mechanisms for Transfer of Applications

Mechanisms for transfer of federally-supported applications have been another, equally important means of implementing federal objectives. In the absence of an appropriate mechanism to "push" or "pull" an application through the various links between research and local use, federal support is likely to prove of little value to local governments. Three primary mechanisms have been employed in the transfer of computer applications: research and demonstration; reporting requirements attached to various federal programs; and subsidies for local application development.

Research and demonstration involves joint federal-local projects intended to create prototype applications suitable for transfer elsewhere. The expectation is that demonstration projects will illustrate clearly the potential benefits of advanced computer applications and thereby "pull" local government practice towards the prototypes without direct federal investment in aiding transfers. Experiments with databanks, urban models, and integrated information systems illustrate early attempts to build prototypes which would be widely transferred. Given the sophistication of these prototypes, it is unclear whether they fit most local situations; given their complexity, it is unclear whether they can be assessed readily by local officials who must make the substantial investments required. More recent demonstrations have involved simpler applications such as uniform fire incident reporting systems, fire station locator, and manpower allocation systems.

Reporting requirements in federal programs, as a method of application transfer, evolved from the tradition of incorporating reporting systems as requirements for local governments receiving funds from federal programs. These previously manual systems are increasingly becoming automated systems which the federal agency develops, packages, and provides to local agencies with a carrot and stick incentive. Local agencies must adopt the automated system if they wish to participate in the program, but the cost of implementing and operating the reporting system is an allowable local expenditure under the program. The benefits of these applications to the local governments are slight since they serve mainly federal purposes, but the costs also appear slight and so local governments adopt these applications. Examples include welfare accounting and reporting systems and transit fare accounting and reporting systems.

Subsidies for local application development, incorporated in categorical grants and revenue-sharing grants, involve the provision of subsidies for local agencies to develop their own applications within broad federal guidelines. Under categorical grants, the only constraints governing development are the nature of the program (e.g., transportation, law enforcement, community development) and the need to demonstrate an association between the information system and the purposes of the categorical grant. Under revenue sharing, local governments can decide for themselves both the purposes and breadth of applications. From the federal perspective, subsidy is an unpredictable mechanism for transfer because local officials might use the categorical or revenue-sharing funds for other purposes than information systems.

STRUCTURE OF THE ANALYSIS

The preceding discussion has served to describe the general technological and policy context for local development of automated information systems. We turn now to a description of an analytic model of technological innovation in local government and of the structure of our analysis.

The model we employ for organizing our analyses can be summarized in terms of "blocks" of variables related to the innovation outcomes. This model is depicted in Fig. 4. The model distinguishes between two sets of variables which constrain and enhance innovation outcomes: innovation attributes and the selection environment. Each of these elements of the model is discussed briefly below.

While most studies of the diffusion of technological innovations take the innovation as a "given," the analytic model we use treats the innovation as an important variant in diffusion and adoption processes. The innovation attributes block in Fig. 4 represents the variable character of innovations as a factor in diffusion processes (Downs & Mohr, 1975). Any innovation is composed of a mix of characteristics which influence its salience to potential adopters (i.e., task complexity, pervasiveness, departure from current technologies and relative cost) and how easily information about it may be communicated (i.e., specificity of evaluation and communicability). The model highlights this fact by explicitly incorporating innovation attributes among the causal variables.

The selection environment consists of factors which may influence the incentives for local governments to adopt an innovation, the availability of information about a particular innovation, and the benefits that can be expected given the innovation's functional capabilities (Nelson & Winter, 1975). As the model in Fig. 4 indicates, the selection environment is composed of extra- as well as intra-organizational elements.

Extra-organization influences are those characteristics which influence the diffusion and transfer of computer applications nationwide within the system of local governments, but which are external to or outside any single local government. Systems characteristics, such as federal policy interventions, may have significant impacts on the diffusion of applications among local governments nationwide and on a local government's decisions to adopt or transfer applications. More proximate subsystem characteristics, such as the networks that exist between local governments, could also have far-reaching implications for the success of resource sharing efforts between local governments. Finally, market characteristics, such as local government cost, technical or behavioral structures, will determine the likelihood that transfer of a computerized innovation will fulfill an organization's need to perform a task with greater rapidity, greater complexity, higher volume, or greater efficiency.

Intra-organizational influences are those characteristics that influence the decisions of individual local governments to adopt computer applications. Characteristics of the immediate local government environment, such as the organizational domain, may be significant causal factors in decisions to adopt or not to adopt new technologies. Staffing and organizational arrangements may be an additional source of decision making influences. Lastly, the existence or lack of executive support for innovation and its effects on decision makers' perceptions of the utility of computing to local government activities may explain differences in the reception of particular applications.

As the model in Fig. 4 suggests, we have also differentiated among several ways of looking at technological innovation processes and their outcomes. Five innovation outcomes, which we have again characterized as extra-or intra-organizational processes, are examined in this book: diffusion, transfer, and resource sharing, which refer to extra-organizational outcomes, and adoptability and adoption, which refer to intra-organizational outcomes. Specifically, diffusion refers to the overall spread of computer applications among local governments. Transfer refers to the process of moving a computer application developed in one local government to another local government. Resource sharing refers to the consolidated use of computing facilities, equipment, and personnel among local governments. Adoptability refers to the probability that an application will be adopted by a local government. Adoption refers to the decision surrounding whether or not a particular computer application will be adopted by a local government.

The book is organized around the model and an investigation of the various innovation processes defined above. It is divided into three parts. Part I takes

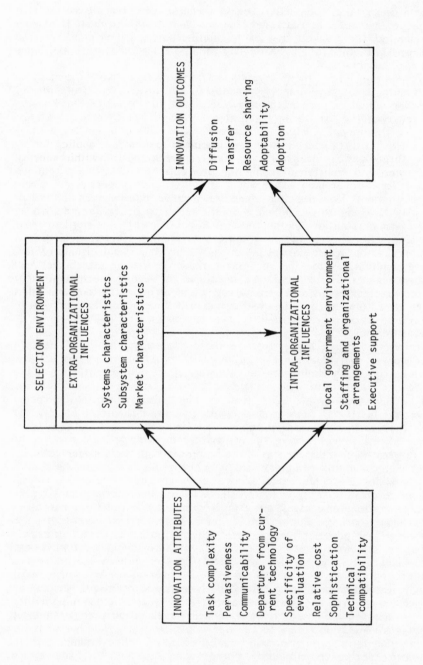

Figure 4. AN ANALYTIC MODEL OF TECHNOLOGICAL INNOVATION IN LOCAL GOVERNMENT

a macro perspective and focuses on the structures influencing diffusion and transfer of computer applications nationwide within the system of local governments. It focuses upon the innovation attributes and the system, subsystem, and market components of the model in Fig. 4. Specifically, Part I examines:

- How innovation attributes and policy interventions affect the extent and rate of application diffusion among local governments (Chapter 1).

- How needs, opportunities and associated costs affect application diffusion, transfer and computing resource sharing within networks of urban governments (Chapter 2).

- How the availability of financial and technical resources and the existence of behavioral characteristics affect the transfer of applications between local governments (Chapter 3).

Part II takes a micro perspective and assesses the decisions of local governments to adopt computer applications. Innovation attributes, local government environment and organization, and the role of the chief executive are the components of the model that are of major interest in these investigations of adoption and adoptability of computer applications. Specifically, Part II examines:

- What characteristics of computer applications and their environment affect the likelihood that one or another innovation will be adopted by a local government (Chapter 4).

- What staffing and organizational arrangements determine the likelihood that computer applications will be adopted by a local government (Chapter 5).

- What determines the likelihood of executive support for computer application adoption in a local government (Chapter 6).

Data for the analyses in these sections were drawn from many sources including: a comprehensive survey of city and county computing characteristics conducted by the Public Policy Research Organization (PPRO) of the University of California, Irvine; the Datapro guide to manufacturers of computers and suppliers of all types of computer related equipment and services; the annual proceedings of the Urban and Regional Information Systems Association (URISA); Datamation; and Computer World. While general descriptions of the variables derived from these data sources are presented within the analyses, more detailed discussions of the measurement of the variables, and of the data sources themselves, are contained in Appendices 1 and 2.

Part III is devoted to a summary and assessment of the findings from the preceding chapters. Of particular importance in Part III is an assessment of the effectiveness of the federal policy interventions discussed in this chapter.

I
Diffusion of Computer Applications Among Local Governments

1 The Influence of Innovation Attributes and Policy Interventions*

As a first step in exploring the "macro" antecedents of innovation diffusion, this chapter focuses on an examination of the relationships between the invariant characteristics of applications, or innovation attributes, systemwide diffusion-related activities, or policy interventions, and diffusion outcomes. In addressing these aspects, the methodology takes account of several criticisms of diffusion research. Among these criticisms are the selection bias of many diffusion studies and the futility of curve fitting as an adequate test of theoretical relevance. To avoid these weaknesses of traditional research, a cluster analysis is used to group the diffusion patterns of applications. These groups of diffusion patterns are then used as an outcome variable to test directly a number of hypotheses on the effects of innovation attributes and policy on diffusion.

Diffusion research(1) has "spread" in recent years from its traditional locus in sociology to the disciplines of economics and political science, and has also begun to move from the investigation of a set of "reasonably narrow and well-defined situations" toward the investigation of more complex and less well-defined settings (Warner, 1974: 434). A selection of new settings studied, from numerous examples, includes: the transfer of aerospace and

---

*This is a revised version of James L. Perry and Kenneth L. Kraemer, "Innovation Attributes, Policy Intervention, and the Diffusion of Computer Applications Among Local Governments," which appeared in Policy Sciences, Vol. 9 (April 1978), pp. 179-205. It is reprinted by permission of the Elsevier Scientific Publishing Company.

defense technologies to local governments (Lambright & Teich, 1974), the spread of public policy innovations among the states (Walker, 1969; Gray, 1973), and the diffusion of advanced technology among state and local mission-oriented agencies (Feller & Menzel, 1976; Feller, Menzel, & Engel, 1974).

This broadening of the scope of diffusion research suggests opportunities for a more complete understanding of the topic area. However, a lack of integration of treatment and of a refined methodology have raised serious obstacles to this goal. Diffusion research is at present a field of research about which Warner (1974: 434) has commented: ". . . even if interdisciplinary research managed to incorporate the diverse findings and approaches into a unified whole . . . social science's understanding of diffusion processes, processes of change, would remain unsatisfactory."

Within the context of our examination of the relationships between diffusion outcomes, innovation attributes, and the selection environment, this analysis takes Warner's criticism as its starting point. Other recent criticisms of diffusion research also are reviewed as a means of formulating the conceptual framework and methodology used in this chapter.

Critiques of Diffusion Research

Recent critiques by Warner (1974), Downs and Mohr (1975), and Rogers (1975) form the foundation for our analysis of some of the deficiencies of diffusion research.(2) Although many of the criticisms of diffusion research have considerable merit, a distinction is made between whether these criticisms involve unexplored empirical issues or unresolved (and possible unresolvable) conceptual and theoretical issues. For instance, Warner's (1974: 441) criticism that "there are no adequate general definitions which offer common ground for the operationalizing of concepts for research purposes" represents an issue that is not likely to be resolved soon, given the variety of disciplines and multiplicity of types of innovations involved in diffusion research. Our review identifies four issues worthy of attention because of the light they might shed upon the more intractable issues. These are selection bias, innovation attributes, origin of the innovation, and the value of curve fitting.

The criticism of diffusion research most frequently voiced concerns selection bias. Downs and Mohr (1975: 46) note in their analysis of current research approaches:

> We also believe that the ubiquitousness of S-shaped diffusion curves is partially an artifact of the kinds of innovations that are usually studied. For the most part, these have consisted of fairly unambiguous technological advances which eventually diffused to most of the population. Yet clearly there are innovations which are not ultimately successful in diffusing through the entire population, but just "fizzle out" after a flurry of early adoptions.

Biased selection of innovations poses two major problems for unravelling the nature of diffusion processes. First, it ignores the possible contingent conditions that differentiate between the "take-off" and spread of a successful innovation and a similar, but non-diffusing, innovation. For policymakers interested in intervening in technological change processes, knowledge about these contingencies is frequently the most crucial information for successful policy development. Second, the selection bias of diffusion research also ignores "flops" that do diffuse. Warner (1974: 442) comments: "Economists would respond that flops do not in general diffuse very extensively. While this proposition may hold true for the competitive market cases, its validity in quasi- and non-market arenas is highly suspect; the phenomenon of 'fads' is tremendously important in many fields."

A second common criticism of diffusion research concerns the lack of attention given to the dimensions or characteristics of an innovation, or innovation attributes. Warner (1974: 442) notes that diffusion research has for the most part been characterized by stable and unidimensional views of technology. Some attention has been directed toward conceptualizing characteristics of innovations, but these concepts have seldom become the basis of empirical research.(3) Categorical distinctions are occasionally made between product and process innovations or physical and behavioral innovations; these distinctions usually serve, however, as criteria for innovation selection and not as an explicit variable. A number of empirical studies have also considered the effects of the attributes of an innovation on its diffusion. Most of these studies, however, have been confined to rural sociology(4) and have utilized perceptual measures of innovation attributes.(5)

A third criticism of diffusion research concerns the origins of an innovation. Warner (1974: 445) writes:

... no one has thoroughly examined how the nature of the innovation's sources – its invention, production, promotion – affects the speed and pattern of its adoption. Does a government-sponsored innovation receive the same selling job as a private sector innovation? Do different types of promoters (producers, etc.) have systematically different approaches to selling their product?

The importance of this issue is demonstrated by the attention given to it in recent studies on government innovation. Feller and Menzel (1976) have posited a number of interesting relationships between supplier activity and diffusion patterns among municipal governments. Their interviews with sales and marketing personnel of firms seeking public sector markets for products suggested relationships between diffusion and city size, spatial location, and, to a lesser extent, a city's reputation for innovation. Bingham's (1975b) analysis of innovation in public housing also suggests the need to consider the source of an innovation.

A fourth criticism found in recent reviews of diffusion research concerns the methodological adequacy of diffusion curve analysis. The S-shaped curve found in traditional diffusion research generally has been attributed to the social interaction among adopters and non-adopters over time. Downs and Mohr (1975: 46) observe:

Diffusion curves may strongly suggest that communications-related variables are important for innovation, but they do not demonstrate the importance, nor do they quantify it, especially in relation to causes of other types. We emphasize this because we have observed a recent tendency, especially among political scientists to assume that because the diffusion of a particular innovation takes the shape of an 'S' curve when graphed, a knowledge of the communication network within the adopting population will "explain" the variations in innovativeness.

Gray's (1973) study of the diffusion of public policies among the states is illustrative of some of the assumptions and problems associated with curve fitting.(6) Gray (1973: 1176) suggests that the social interaction explanation of innovation diffusion is the most appealing one on substantive grounds because state government "decisionmakers emulate or take cues from legislation passed by other states." Although Gray (1973: 1176) notes "the futility of curve fitting as a satisfactory test of theoretical relevance," she proceeds to apply a simple interaction model which employs a number of important assumptions. Among the assumptions are that "leaders from each adopter state come in contact with leaders from each nonadopting state" (complete intermixture) and that there is no constant source from which the innovation is diffused (Gray, 1973: 1176).

The latter assumption is particularly suspect given Gray's discussion of some of the welfare policies scrutinized in the study and the reported frequency distributions for their adoption. Diffusion from a constant source appeared to characterize a number of the innovations analyzed, including aid for dependent children and welfare merit system legislation. Gray's assumption that the population is completely intermixed is disputed by Walker (1973: 1187):

> This diffusion process forms an essentially geographical pattern, and can be visualized as a succession of spreading ink-blots on a map created by the initial adoptions of new policies by states playing in a national 'league' of cue taking and information exchange, followed by other states whose standards of comparison and measures of aspiration are more parochial and who typically adopt new policies only after others within their 'league' have done so.

Bingham (1975a) also concludes that there are no national or state patterns of innovation diffusion among local governments.

CONCEPTUAL FRAMEWORK

These foregoing criticisms provide implied directions for research on the diffusion of innovation which are incorporated in our expansion of a portion of the conceptual model (shown in italics in Fig. 5) presented in the Introduction. The framework breaks with traditional diffusion research in several ways. First, as we've noted, its focus on the structural sources (innovation attributes) of variations in diffusion patterns contrasts with most previous frameworks' focus on process considerations. The framework also opens the way for testing alternatives to interactive models of diffusion. It submits several of the assumptions of the interaction model of diffusion to an empirical test.

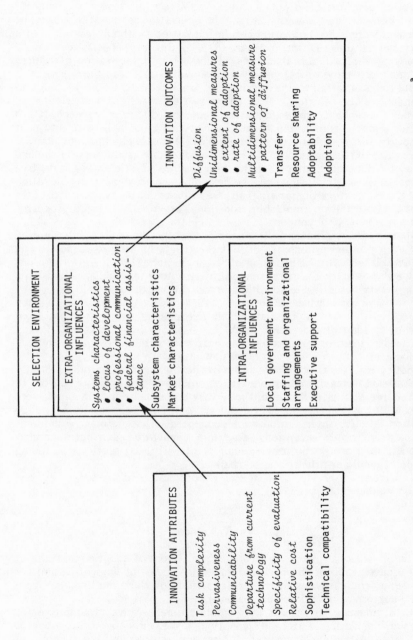

Figure 5. EXPANSION OF THE SYSTEMS CHARACTERISTICS COMPONENT OF THE ANALYTIC MODEL[a]

[a]The variables in italics represent the specific portion of the analytic model examined in this chapter.

Innovation attributes and policy interventions are the sets of explanatory variables used in the analysis (Fig. 5). Innovation attributes represent properties on which the innovation can be classified "without reference to a specified organization" (Downs & Mohr, 1975: 9). Several benefits are derived from studying the primary attributes of innovations. Innovation attributes reflect the multi-dimensional nature of innovations. Thus, they provide a means for characterizing the design of an innovation. Developing an understanding of the relationships of an innovation's "design" or attributes to its diffusion can enhance the explanatory import of diffusion research. It can assist in developing cumulative theory by increasing our ability to interpret the instability across current empirical studies.(7) It also can aid in evaluating strategies for diffusing innovations. If innovation attributes do indeed influence diffusion, then they should be considered when choosing incentive systems to encourage diffusion or when designing or redesigning an innovation for a particular system of potential users. In essence, innovation attributes represent a potentially manipulable, additional aspect of diffusion processes for consideration by policymakers.

The notion of manipulation is encompassed by the policy intervention concept. Policy interventions are activities or sets of activities, public and private, associated with the diffusion of an innovation.(8) Policy interventions may be viewed as attempts "to manage infrastructure (manipulate fields) and in so doing make it desirable for other organizations to behave in ways they would not have otherwise" (Thompson, 1974: 20). Attempts to manage infrastructures may be intentional or unintentional and may emanate from within the system of potential users or from external sources. Policy interventions therefore characterize the activities within the policy environment associated with the diffusion of an innovation.

The policy intervention concept takes explicit account of variables usually left unmeasured in traditional curve fitting studies and of possible sources of constant source diffusion. Because it may vary and is subject to manipulation, the source of an innovation is viewed as only one dimension of policy intervention. Policy intervention as a concept also has normative implications. Since policy interventions are, like innovation attributes, multi-dimensional, their study can provide insight into diffusion tactics – including the choice of public or private sector channels.

The variables used to test these concepts are discussed next and elaborated further in Appendix 1.

Dependent Variables

Two unidimensional measures of diffusion – extent of adoption and rate of adoption – have traditionally been employed in studies of innovation and are used as dependent variables in the present study. A third multi-dimensional measure – pattern of adoption – also is used.

Extent of adoption represents the cumulative percentage of adoptions for a particular innovation. Extent of adoption is measured by the number of adopters of a particular computer application divided by the number of useable responses to the survey.

Rate of adoption is defined by Rogers and Shoemaker (1971: 154) as:

. . . the relative speed with which the innovation is adopted by members of a social system. Thus, rate of adoption is usually measured by the length of time required for a certain percentage of the members of a system to adopt an innovation.

While rate of adoption for the Rogers and Shoemaker measure is expressed in years, Fliegel and Kivlin (1966) employ a measure based on the number of adoptions per year.(9) Each is a valid measure of the relative speed at which an innovation is adopted, but each might actually measure a different part of a diffusion curve. If that is indeed the case, the results obtained from using these two measures of rate of adoption may vary considerably. Based upon the perspective that both are valid measures of rate of adoption, two specific measures for the rate of adoption of computer applications were developed. The first measure is the number of years for a computer application to diffuse to three percent of the local government population. The second measure is the number of adoptions of computer applications per year over the ten consecutive years of most rapid adoption for that application.

Pattern of adoption represents the overall pattern of diffusion formed by the extent and rate of diffusion and the time of introductoin of an innovation.(10) It is a multi-dimensional outcome variable for local government computer applications formed by cluster analysis of six variables that describe the diffusion pattern of each application. The six variables used in the cluster analysis were: mean year of adoption, standard deviation (in years) of the adoption distribution, peakedness (kurtosis) of the distribution, skewness, range (in years) of the adoption period, and the cumulative percentage of adoptions.

Ten patterns of adoption were identified for the population of applications from the cluster analysis. These patterns are presented in Table 1. Among the diffusion patterns are the standard S-curve cumulative frequency distributions (clusters 7, 9), several of which suggest the likelihood of constant source diffusion (clusters 5, 6, 8), and several of which are indicative of non-diffusing innovations (clusters 1, 2, 3). Cluster 10 in Table 1 includes all those applications ($N = 95$) which have only recently been introduced into the local government system

Independent Variables

The literature suggests six innovation attributes that might be expected to be related to diffusion. These are: task complexity, pervasiveness, communicability, specificity of evaluation, departure from current technologies, and cost. Each is explained next, and the operational definitions are presented in Appendix 2.

Task complexity refers to the complexity of implementing different information processing tasks.(11) It distinguishes "the primary attribute of the information processing involved in a given activity" and "might be a basis for predicting the differential effect of automating activities in terms of their impacts for operational performance, decision making, and the municipal work environment" (Kraemer, Dutton, & Matthews, 1975: 6). At the very least we would expect that the different couplings of men and machines which

TABLE 1.   COMPUTER APPLICATION DIFFUSION PATTERNS AMONG LOCAL GOVERNMENTS

Cluster   Narrative   _____ Frequency
Number   Description ....Cumulative Frequency

NUMBER OF
ADOPTIONS

1. Occasional adoption during the period, but extremely limited diffusion.

   N = 15

TIME

2. Minimal diffusion with most adoptions occurring early in the period.

   N = 6

3. Minimal diffusion with first adoptions about mid-way during the period.

   N = 17

4. Limited diffusion with first adoptions beginning early in the period.

   N = 26

5. Limited diffusion, beginning about mid-way in the period, with a brief span of rapid adoption near the end of the period.

   N = 50

6. Moderate diffusion with a brief flurry of adoption near the end of the period.

   N = 18

7. Moderate diffusion with adoption beginning early in the period and continueing at a relatively constant level.

   N = 8

8. Extensive diffusion with rapid adoption occurring near the end of the period.

   N = 8

9. Extensive diffustion with first adoptions early in the period and adoption continuing at a high level through most of the period.

   N = 12

10. Incomplete diffusion with first adoptions occurring late in the period.

    N = 95

these information processing tasks represent are more difficult to implement because they place different demands on an organization's social system efficiency.(12) As implementation becomes more difficult, diffusion might be expected to decrease.

Pervasiveness refers to the "degree to which an innovation relates to and requires changes or adjustments on the part of other elements" in the organization (Lin & Zaltman, 1973: 103). In this study, pervasiveness measures the generality or specificity of the use of an application within an organization. We expect that this innovation attribute would affect how organizational actors perceive an innovation's contribution to the organization and its impact on budgetary allocations.

Communicability of an innovation represents one aspect of "the degree to which the results of an innovation are visible to others" (Rogers & Shoemaker, 1971: 155). The extent of documentation of a computer application is used here to measure the communicability of an application outside its system of users or developers. We would expect that computer applications that are documented sufficiently so they can be transferred easily to another organizational setting will exhibit greater diffusion than those applications with insufficient documentation.

Specificity of evaluation is the degree to which an innovation's output can be measured objectively. Woodward (1970: 35) argues that a "causal link between technology and organizational behavior is the degree of uncertainty and unpredictability in the production task." Honnold and Erickson (1974) suggest that specificity of evaluation is a measure of uncertainty about the instrumental value of a technological change. Therefore, we expect that greater specificity of evaluation would enhance the diffusion of applications.

Departure from current technologies refers to the relative differences between newly developed technologies and technologies presently used by organizations in the focal system. When a technology is first introduced into the local government system, how different is it from existing technologies, and how does this difference affect its diffusion? Does the "newness" of a technology detract from or enhance its diffusion? Generally, we expect that the greater the departure of an application from technologies in use, the greater the likelihood that it will be less compatible with current system requirements and therefore less acceptable to potential users, at least initially. However, the fact that an application was developed may be prima facie evidence of potentially significant need for the application within the system of users, and therefore it might be more acceptable later despite its current incompatibility.

The relative cost of implementing an innovation is the final attribute examined. In the absence of profitability or return on investment criteria for government organizations, the cost of implementation may be the single most important economic variable in the public sector innovation process. Applications were coded according to whether the cost of implementing the application relative to other applications within a particular department was low, moderate, or high. Although the role of cost has received little explicit attention in studies of public sector innovation, we would expect that the greater the costs of implementing a computer application, the less likely it will be diffused widely.

The literature on innovation also suggests three policy interventions which are considered: locus of development, professional communication, and the availability of federal financial assistance.

Locus of development, notably absent in previous diffusion research, reflects one aspect of an innovation's origin. It refers to the four alternative sources of development of local government computer applications software: federal agencies, manufacturers, other non-local-government sources, and local governments themselves. The primary distinguishing feature of these four sources is their centralization vis-a-vis the local government system. Federal sources are viewed as the most centralized sources of development, local governments as the most decentralized sources of development. We expect that the more centralized the source of the innovation, the more likely there will be constant source diffusion, and therefore the greater the diffusion.

Professional communication, a second policy which would influence diffusion, refers to the amount of communication about an application within professional channels. Professional communications media provide a major means of disseminating information on recent technological developments, assessments of particular technologies, and specific experiences with an application. Communication within such professional networks is measured by the number of published articles on an application in three diverse professional publications, the URISA Proceedings, Datamation, and Computer World.

Availability of federal assistance for the implementation (development or transfer) of computer applications is the third policy investigated. Federal financial assistance is measured as a dichotomous variable indicating either that no assistance was available for implementation of a given application, or that federal assistance was available. The level of federal assistance to state and local governments for automated information systems, estimated conservatively around $250 million annually (Davis, 1972), is sufficiently large that it could reasonably be expected to positively influence the diffusion of computer applications. However, restrictions placed upon the use of some federal funds might dampen the diffusion of some applications. The Law Enforcement Assistance Administration, for example, required until recently that its project grants be spent only for law enforcement applications on computers dedicated to such applications and operated by uniformed personnel. Furthermore, federal investment frequently is directed towards costly and difficult to implement computer applications such as those assocated with the USAC demonstration projects (Kraemer, 1971).

RESEARCH METHODOLOGY

Two types of analysis were performed in assessing the relationships between innovation attributes, policy interventions, and the diffusion of computer applications among local governments: multiple regression and discriminant analysis. These analyses were based on an N of 112.

Multiple regression techniques were used to analyze the relationships between the independent variables and three unidimensional measures of diffusion: 1) the extent of adoption, 2) the rate of adoption as indicated by the "number of applications adopted per year over the ten most active years of adoption," and 3) the rate of adoption as indicated by the "number of years for the application to diffuse to three percent of the population." The expected relationships between the innovation attributes, policy interventions and extent and rate of adoption are summarized in Table 2. Signs in the table represent the expected direction of the relationships between the operational indicators. Since the two operational measures of rate of adoption are inversely related (e.g., a high number of adoptions per year and a low number of years to diffuse each reflect rapid adoption), the opposite signs for the rate of adoption relationships in Table 2 reflect equivalent relationships. In the regression analyses we controlled for distortion caused by some applications being in the early stages of diffusion by using only cases falling in Clusters 1-9 of Table 1, i.e., those which had diffused.

Table 2. EXPECTED RELATIONSHIPS BETWEEN THE INNOVATION ATTRIBUTES, POLICY INTERVENTIONS, AND EXTENT AND RATE OF ADOPTION OF COMPUTER APPLICATIONS

Independent Variables	Extent of Adoption	Rate of Adoption	
	Cumulative percentage of adoptions for an application	Number of applications adopted per 10 most active years of adoption	Number of years for the application to diffuse to 3% of the population
INNOVATION ATTRIBUTES			
Task complexity	-	-	+
Pervasiveness	+	+	-
Communicability	+	+	-
Departure from current technologies	-	-	+
Specificity of evaluation	+	+	-
Cost relative to other agency applications	-	-	+
POLICY INTERVENTION			
Locus of development	-	-	+
Professional communication	+	+	-
Federal financial assistance	+	+	-

Discriminant analysis was used to identify relationships between innovation attributes, policy interventions, and the multi-dimensional measure of diffusion – the pattern of adoption. The intent of the analysis was to relate diffusion outcomes (represented by the nine groups in Table 1) to the design of the innovation and the role of policy. Discriminant functions allow us to assess which innovation attributes pose the greatest constraints to computer application diffusion and which policies might be most effective for diffusing particular types of applications.

Whereas the multiple regression analysis attempted to obtain a best fit between a criterion variable and a set of predictors, the purpose of the discriminant analysis was to distinguish among groups of cases using variables on which the groups are hypothesized to differ. The nine patterns of adoption of computer applications (Table 1) served as the criterion variable. In computing the first discriminant functions, all nine groups were used as the criterion and an F-test was computed for the distance measure between groups. The F-ratios indicated that the distance between groups 1, 2 and 3 and between groups 6 and 7 were not significantly different for the predictor variables.   Thus, these five groups were combined into two groups and a second set of discriminant functions were derived using only six criterion groups. The results of the discriminant analysis for each of the criterion groupings (i.e., the six and nine groupings) were not substantially different, and therefore the results are reported only for six criterion groups.

RESEARCH FINDINGS

Multiple Regression Analysis

The regression results for each of the diffusion indicators are presented in Table 3. One general observation about the regressions, which we suggested earlier, is that the two operational indicators of rate of adoption appear to measure different aspects of diffusion curves. For example, departure from current technologies is positively associated with both the number of adoptions per year (indicating the greater the departure, the more rapid the diffusion during peak adoption years) and the number of years taken for the application to diffuse to three percent of the population (indicating the greater the departure, the less rapid the diffusion during the initial years of diffusion). The differences in these two measures point to one possible reason for the inconsistency in previous diffusion findings.(13) These differences also confirm the value of using either multiple indicators or multi-dimensional indicators as dependent variables in diffusion studies.

The expected ralationships between three innovation attributes – departure from current technologies, pervasiveness and specificity of evaluation – are supported by the regression equation. Departure from current technologies is highly significant in each equation. The positive association with the cumulative extent of adoption indicates that an application's initial status vis-a-vis other technologies actually has a positive impact on its acceptance by local governments. The positive association with both rate of adoption measures indicates that an application's departure from existing technologies has a dampening effect on its adoption in the initial stages of diffusion but has a positive effect during the peak years.

Table 3. MULTIPLE LINEAR REGRESSIONS FOR EXTENT AND RATE OF COMPUTER APPLICATION ADOPTION

Independent Variables	Extent of Adoption	Rate of Adoption	
	Cumulative percentage of adoptions for an application	Number of applications adopted per 10 most active years of adoption	Number of years for the application to diffuse to 3% of the population
INNOVATION ATTRIBUTES			
Task complexity	.00	.02	.10
Pervasiveness	.38***	.38***	-.06
Communicability	-.06	-.06	.08
Departure from current technologies	.29***	.24***	.49***
Specificity of evaluation	.25**	.29**	.08
Cost relative to other agency applications	.08	.11	-.22**
POLICY INTERVENTIONS			
Locus of development	-.09	-.03	-.06
Professional communication	.12	.13	.10
Federal financial assistance	-.10	-.09	-.19*
Constant	-.03	-8.03	8.58
R^2	.36	.33	.29
F	6.43***	6.11***	4.76***

* $p < .05$
** $p < .025$
*** $p < .01$

Pervasiveness and specificity of evaluation have strong positive associations with two of the measures of adoption (extent and peak rate of adoption). Cost, on the other hand, is non-significant in these two regressions, but it positively influences the initial rate of adoption. This later finding reinforces Fliegel and Kivlin's (1966) conclusion that cost per se is not a significant negative influence on the rate of adoption. This suggests that it probably is necessary to consider cost relative to some perceived or anticipated benefit in order to adequately specify the independent variable. Unlike cost, pervasiveness and specificity of evaluation are significant and influence the likelihood of successful adoption. The collective results of these three attributes suggest that some broader concepts such as risk and uncertainty might underlie differences in the diffusion of computer applications.

It is noteworthy that pervasiveness is positively and significantly associated with extent of adoption and the number of adoptions per year, but not significantly related to the rate of adoption in the initial years. This suggests that certain applications in areas such as finance are highly valued candidates for automation because they are multi-functional or organization-wide. One would therefore expect a high number of adoptions overall. But the multi-function nature of these applications means that implementation is complex and difficult. Therefore, the initial rate of diffusion is slow. Once appropriate "model applications" have been developed, their adoption might be quite rapid. Of course, it also is possible that their adoption will remain slow precisely because they are organization-wide in scope.

Communicability is non-significant in all of the regressions. It should be emphasized again that our definition and measurement of the concept is very different from that in most of the literature. The literature refers to the ease of others understanding both the operational and performance aspects of the application. Our measure simply taps the availability of one highly technical form of communication. Yet, the measure of communicability is related to both practice and policy. Practitioners argue that documentation is essential for transfer. Federal and state officials require local governments to document programs developed with their financial aid in order to facilitate transfer. Therefore, the fact that documentation is non-significantly but negatively associated with each of the diffusion measures has practical importance.

Few of the expected relationships between the policy variables and the dependent variables are substantiated by the regression equations. The strongest relationship is that between financial aid and initial diffusion (the number of years for the application to diffuse to three percent of the population). The relationships between professional communication and the dependent variables are significant at about the .10 level. Locus of development is unrelated. Federal financial assistance appears to have a positive influence in reducing the time span for the initial diffusion of an application. The overall pattern of relationships for federal assistance is consistent with the possible impacts of one type of federal diffusion strategy. The federal government has funded experiments for some applications as a way of demonstrating feasibility and utility. Following limited experimentation and transfer, these federal diffusion efforts are then discontinued on the grounds that normal market mechanisms will prove adequate to complete the diffusion process. Thus, initial diffusion may be speeded, but the long-run rate and extent of adoption may be unaffected.

One reason for the weak relationships between policy variables and diffusion is that policies may not be independent of an innovation's attributes. Particular types of innovations, either because of their implications for advancing the use of the technology or because of their attractiveness from a purely technical standpoint, probably have higher potential for receiving attention in professional circles than other types of innovations. Similarly, federal support may be directed at applications which are difficult to diffuse among local governments. Three multiplicative terms were entered into the separate regressions to test for this type of interaction: federal assistance x task complexity, professional communication x departure from current technologies, and cost x federal assistance. The addition of these terms led to some improvement in the R^2s, but none significantly improved the overall prediction of variance. However, it is possible that functional specifications different from those we used might improve the regression results.

Discriminant Analysis

The results of the discriminant analysis are shown in Table 4.(14) Two significant functions were derived when using innovation attributes and policy as the discriminating variables.(15)

In the first discriminant function (Table 4, column 1), the magnitudes of the coefficients indicate that the primary determinants of group membership are departure from existing technologies and federal financial assistance. The opposite direction of the association for these two variables is worth noting. Federal financial assistance is positively associated with group membership, which means that the higher the group score, generally, the more extensive and/or rapid the diffusion. Departure from existing technologies is negatively associated with group membership, which means that the lower the group score, generally, the less extensive and less rapid the diffusion. This first function can be termed systemic facilitation since the two significant variables are identifying the departure of the application from other technologies in use within the system, and the availability to all local governments of federal resources for designing and implementing the application.

In the second discriminant function, four variables are about equally significant: pervasiveness, departure from existing technologies, specificity of evaluation, and federal financial assistance. Although federal assistance differs in kind from the other three variables, we term this discriminating dimension attribute facilitation. It indicates that the more pervasive, evaluable, and novel the application, the more likely it will be a member of one of the diffusion groups characterized by extensive and rapid adoption.

In addition to providing information on significant factors in the diffusion process, the discriminant functions can also be tested for their ability to classify known group members, i.e., those which have diffused. Table 5 presents the predicted group membership of the applications using the functions derived from the innovation attribute and policy variables. Table 6 identifies the applications in each cell of Table 5. The ability of the discriminant functions to classify known group members essentially reflects

Table 4. DISCRIMINANT FUNCTIONS FOR THE INNOVATION ATTRIBUTES AND POLICY
          INTERVENTIONS

	Function 1	Function 2
INNOVATION ATTRIBUTES		
Task complexity	.19	.14
Pervasiveness	-.10	.58
Communicability	-.14	-.31
Departure from existing techniques	-.55	.45
Specificity of evaluation	-.11	.58
Relative agency cost	-.22	.18
POLICY INTERVENTIONS		
Locus of development	.19	.00
Professional communication	.16	.00
Federal financial assistance	.77	.51
Eigenvalue	.68	.32
Canonical correlation	.64	.49
Wilks' lambda	.67*	.89*

* Significant at $X^2 < .05$

the extent to which the discriminating variables separate the cases into
mutually exclusive groups. Applications with known group membership are
correctly classified in 44 percent of the cases.

The discriminant functions also provide a means for classifying cases with
unknown group membership, i.e., those which have not yet diffused very
much. Applications in Group 7 were initially distinguished from the other
applications because they were in the early stages of diffusion and could not
be grouped with those applications that had diffused significantly. However,
these cases can be classified according to the diffusion group in which they
will eventually fall using the values of the cases on the discriminating
variables. The predicted group membership of the 95 applications in Group 7
is displayed at the bottom of Table 5.

Table 5. DIFFUSION GROUP MEMBERSHIP OF THE COMPUTER APPLICATIONS PREDICTED BY THE DISCRIMINANT FUNCTIONS FOR THE SIX GROUP CRITERION

Actual Group	# of Cases	Predicted group membership					
		Group 1	Group 2	Group 3	Group 4	Group 5	Group 6
DIFFUSING APPLICATIONS[a]							
Group 1 (Clusters 1, 2 and 3 in Table 1)	38	31 81.6%	1 2.6%	5 13.2%	1 2.6%	0 0.0%	0 0.0%
Group 2 (Cluster 4)	26	7 26.9	2 7.7	17 65.4	0 0.0	0 0.0	1 0.0
Group 3 (Cluster 5)	50	14 28.0	6 12.0	24 48.0	5 10.0	0 0.0	1 2.0
Group 4 (Clusters 6 and 7)	26	7 26.9	0 0.0	10 38.5	5 19.2	1 3.8	3 11.5
Group 5 (Cluster 8)	8	0 0.0	0 0.0	4 50.0	0 0.0	4 50.0	0 0.0
Group 6 (Cluster 9)	12	3 25.0	0 0.0	0 0.0	4 33.3	0 0.0	5 41.7
NON-DIFFUSING APPLICATIONS[b]							
Group 7 (Cluster 10)	95	5 5.3%	39 41.1%	29 30.5%	1 1.1%	21 22.1%	0 0.0%

[a] Percent of grouped cases (Groups 1-6) correctly classified is 44.38%

[b] Predicted group membership for those applications which are in the early stages of/diffusion.

Table 6. COMPUTER APPLICATIONS INCLUDED IN THE DIFFUSION GROUPS

ACTUAL GROUP MEMBERSHIP	PREDICTED GROUP MEMBERSHIP 1	2	3	4	5	6
1	Building ID & location file; Deed records; Land, plat records; Animal Control: code violation records; Traffic light control; Traffic control device inv.; Traffic light maintenance scheduling; Traffic flow projections; Solid Waste: equipment and manpower allocation; Refuse collection scheduling; Liquid Waste: equipment and manpower allocation; Location of water facilities; Water production records; Elec.: inventory and location files; Elec.: customer inquiry; Elec.: consumption data; Gas: utility accounting; Gas: customer inquiry; Gas: consumption data; Health certificates/permits file; Health inspection records; Insect & rodent inspection; Caseworker & social worker case records; Public housing assistance data; Records on distribution of clothing, eyeglasses, etc.; Birth records; Death records; Marriage records; Divorce records; Adoption records; Library: periodical holdings	Water: customer inquiry	Permits: safety licenses; Traffic flow data; Elec.: utility billing; Elec.: utility accounting; Gas: utility billing	Welfare: program case records (Homemakers, Neighborhood service center, other local agencies)		
2	Purchasing: bid file; DP: data dictionary; Space utilization records; Streets and highways maintenance records and schedules; Immunization records; Parks and recreation facility inventory; Automatic precincting	Engineering design calculations; Health education records	Field interrogation report file; Firearms registration file; Building description records; Building inspection records; Plaintiff/defendant records; Probation records; Federal & State grant files; Regression for residential property appraisals; Regression for non-residential property appraisals; Model cities information system; Substandard structure reports; Building complaint records; Design requirement files; Construction records and scheduling; Water pollution monitoring and records; Patient medical and treatment records; Cemetery records			

34

	Modus operandi	Criminal offense file	Cash management/cash flow analysis	Budget preparation	Accounting: cost accounting	General accounting
3	Bonded debt & interest accounting; Securities & funds records; Purchasing: requisition file; Purchasing: central stores file; Commodity price record file; Collective bargaining, labor negotiations support; Data processing: debugging routines; Building maintenance records; Print shop job file; Animal licenses; Streets and highways inventory, location; Solid waste billing; Water: vehicle maintenance records	Modus operandi; Commercial business activity and sales; Right of way file; Parks & recreation accounting; Vote counting; Vote auditing	Criminal offense file; Juvenile criminal offense file; Alias name file; Stolen vehicles file; Motor vehicles registration file; Fire apparatus inventory file; Courtroom calendars and scheduling; Court docketing; Court disposition file; Child support records; Expenditure forecasting; Revenue forecasting; Media mailing list; Telephone directory; Land use inventory file; Solid waste accounting; AFDC records; Aid to blind records; Aid to disabled records; Old age assistance records; Food stamp records	Cash management/cash flow analysis; Sales ratio analysis; Water: inventory & location files; General assistance records; Circulation records/overdue notices			General accounting
4	Business license records; Calculation of real property value, assessing; Purchasing: vendor file; Computer utilization records; Peripheral equipment utilization; Water: utility accounting; Water: consumption data		Uniform Crime Reporting (UCR); Parking ticket file; Traffic violations file; Wants/warrants file; Preparation of vouchers, warrants for city funds; Budget monitoring; Position Classification listing; Data Processing: Job acct'g listing; Voter registration records; Voter mailing list	Non-property tax records and billing; Tax maps; Purchase order file; Position control (budget as actual); Employee records	Budget preparation	Accounting: cost accounting; Motor vehicle equipment file; Motor vehicle maintenance records	
5			Arrest records; Traffic accident file; Vehicle maintenance records; Jury selection		Other crime reporting system; Police: service data (Type of call, location, etc.); Program budget preparation; Budgeting: program structure rel. to line-to-line budget		
6	Check reconciliation; Tax roll, listing of all property; Property ownership list			Property tax records/billing; Special assessment and tax records; Data processing: customer billing; Water: utility billing		Check preparing/issuing; Payroll prep./acct'g; Retirement/pension records; Real property records; Personal property records	

Summary

The findings of the regression analysis and discriminant analysis were essentially similar. However, the discriminant analysis provides a more complete picture of the diffusion of computer application in local governments. Discriminant analysis indicated that the diffusion of computer applications is facilitated by both the attributes of the application and system characteristics. This duality of discriminating dimensions may explain some of the lack of consistency in the findings of previous studies on the effect of perceived attributes on innovation diffusion. While the attribute facilitation dimension clearly demonstrated that innovation attributes are significant factors in the diffusion of innovations, the discriminating power of the systemic facilitation dimension indicated that factors independent of an innovation's attributes are sufficient for diffusion.

The structure of the innovation attribute and policy discriminant functions raises some questions about underlying causal processes which, although they cannot be answered here, are worth noting. For example, several causal processes might be plausible given the structure of the attribute facilitation function. One underlying causal process could be described as "need-based." The magnitudes and directions of the variables on the attribute facilitation function could be the result of felt needs, search, and adoption among some system members, and subsequent diffusion to other system members with similar felt needs. This appears to us to be the most plausible underlying causal process. If it is, it suggests that the local government system could be an efficient network in assessing and meeting needs for innovation. This optimistic assessment is tempered by the fact that the importance of the pervasiveness and evaluability attributes may also point to a predisposition toward risk minimizing behavior among local government officials.

Alternative causal processes may also underlie the systemic facilitation functions. For example, motivated by the availability of federal funding for local use in developing new computer applications, private entrepreneurs may enter the market and encourage local governments to implement incremental adjustments to their existing technologies. On the other hand, local officials may see the availability of federal funds as an opportunity to add new data processing capabilities to areas in which they have previously undertaken considerable systems development. Although the discriminant functions provide a framework within which to consider policy alternatives, the underlying causal mechanisms require further investigation.

DISCUSSION

From a research perspective, this analysis offers several interesting implications. We initially noted that Rogers (1975) and others (Downs & Mohr, 1975; Warner, 1974) have criticized researchers for selection bias, i.e., their propensity to select only widely diffusing innovations. In contrast, our population of computer applications included both diffusing and non-diffusing applications. One way of assessing the implications of our selection criterion is to consider two results of this analysis that differ from the results of studies that used only widely diffusing innovations. We found that the communicability of an innovation and communication with professional circles had no significant impact on the diffusion of computer application among local governments, a finding contrary to the large majority of previous studies. We also found that the availability of federal financial assistance helps to differentiate diffusing from non-diffusing innovations, contrary to Yin, et al.'s (1976) study of state and local innovations. These differences could, of course, be the result of the set of innovations we studied. However, the possibility that excluding non-diffusing innovations from diffusion research has led to ascribing significance to important variables in the diffusion process clearly cannot be discounted by the results of this analysis. Further research exploring both diffusing and non-diffusing innovations will be necessary before any firm conclusions can be reached on which variables from previous research are truly significant factors in diffusion.

As suggested by Warner (1974), our analysis indicates that innovation attributes do play a significant role in an innovation's diffusion. The discriminant analysis indicated, however, that facilitative attributes are sufficient, but probably not necessary, conditions for innovation diffusion.

Our investigation of the effects of the origin of the innovation on diffusion was limited to assessing the effect of locus of development. The analysis of local government computer applications showed no relationship between locus of development and diffusion patterns. No source of development seems to occupy a "favored" status in the local government computer application market. Because the sources of data processing technology and expertise are relatively extensive compared to other public sector technologies, this finding might be generalizable to other technologies in local government.

The value of curve fitting in diffusion research also was questioned. Our analysis departed from that traditional methodology in favor of using cluster analysis to identify alternative diffusion curves and discriminant analysis to identify key variables in the diffusion process. Several of the diffusion patterns derived from the population of local government computer applications deviated from the S shaped model and several also suggested the likelihood of constant source for diffusion. The significance of federal financial assistance in the discriminant functions supported the constant source explanation.

From a policy perspective, this analysis also offers several guidelines for future action. The analysis suggests that to maximize its effectiveness federal support of computing (and probably other local government technologies) must adapt to contingencies created by differences in technologies and changing circumstances as well as take advantage of opportunities to manipulate key variables in the diffusion process. The major contingencies facing federal intervention appear to be when to initiate and when to withdraw support, and for what purposes. Federal financial assistance is likely to be most successful (success being defined in terms of both the diffusion group membership of a technology and the fulfillment of local needs) if it is directed toward technologies which represent a breakthrough from technologies in use and which possess attributes attractive to the target population. Accomplishing this will require some vision for identifying "innovative" technologies with attributes to which local government officials would be responsive. Although this strategy might be successful, it may not be cost effective. Even in the absence of federal assistance, technologies with attributes attractive to system members could be expected to diffuse widely and relatively quickly. Furthermore, assuming that federal objectives may differ or even conflict with local objectives, federal officials are likely to sacrifice the achievement of federal objectives in choosing innovations with attributes that facilitate diffusion and contribute to local government objectives.

In any event, thorough analysis of the local government market would appear to be a prerequisite of federal support. Such an analysis must not only explore the ways in which local government technologies are deficient, but it must also explore local government needs, responsiveness to particular technologies, and responsiveness to various types of incentives. When federal objectives for the development of a new technology differ from local objectives, a two-stage program of federal support may be the most effective strategy for intervention. The first stage would emphasize the development of local capabilities in areas related to the technology. The second stage would be directed at technologies that enhance federal objectives, but build local capabilities developed during the first stage.

CONCLUSION

Federal financial assistance, innovation attributes, and local government needs may be better predictors of the diffusion of computer applications than interaction among adopters and non-adopters. Furthermore, the discriminant analysis indicated the plausibility of alternative processes of diffusion occurring within the same population of adopters.

At a more general level, our analysis suggests a need for greater emphasis on structural variables in diffusion research, the development of alternatives to sequential models of the diffusion process, and the use of diverse methodologies in building diffusion theory. Development of greater diversity within the field holds promise of increasing the richness of diffusion theory, improving our understanding of diffusion processes, and identifying effective strategies for policy intervention.

2 The Influence of Cooperation in Urban Intergovernmental Networks on Diffusion, Transfer, and Resource Sharing*

Since local governments must maintain some formal or informal relationships with other proximate local governments, these networks constitute a widespread and important subsystem of policy interventions that may influence patterns of innovation diffusion. In this chapter, dependent outcome variables measuring the rate of diffusion, transfer, and resource sharing are used to assess the influences of organizations' need for interdependence, opportunities for cooperation, and the costs associated with network arrangements.

In recent years, there has been increasing interest in the potentials that formal or informal relationships between proximate local governments offer for the spread of technological innovations. City-county consolidation (Rosenbaum & Henderson, 1973) and interjurisdictional service agreements (Friesma, 1970) are among the forms of urban intergovernmental cooperation that have sprouted as means of improving the economy, efficiency, and effectiveness of local governments in the face of increasing governmental fragmentation, service duplication, and uncoordinated urban change.

Within the context of local government computing, intergovernmental cooperation has been encouraged for a number of reasons. First, since computing in local governments is a relatively new development, cooperation among governmental units has been encouraged as a means of speeding the

*This is a revised version of James L. Perry, "Cooperation in Urban Intergovernmental Networks and the Diffusion and Transfer of Computer Applications," which appeared in Urban Analysis, Vol. 5 (1978), pp. 111-129. It is reprinted by permission of Gordon and Breach Science Publishers Ltd.

diffusion of the use of computing. This is particularly apparent in federal agencies' and professional groups' advocacy of the transfer of computer applications software among local governments (Kraemer, 1977). Second, the use and effectiveness of some local government computer applications require intergovernmental cooperation. For example, the U.S. Census Bureau's Geographic Base File-Dual Independent Map Encoding (GBF-DIME) application is designed for use primarily by multi-governmental units (Rogers & Eveland, 1976). Finally, the relative cost of computer hardware and the application of computing to particular governmental uses is often high enough that urban intergovernmental cooperation may be the only means by which it can be economically implemented.

Despite interest in intergovernmental cooperation from a prescriptive viewpoint, however, little significant progress has been made in understanding its influence on innovation diffusion or other processes (Reid, 1972; Schermerhorn, 1975). Our primary interest in this analysis is to address this gap by exploring the antecedents of different types of urban intergovernmental cooperation in local government computing. Interorganizational theory serves as the conceptual foundation of the analysis and empirical study.

Interorganizational Theory

Interorganizational theory has provided the organizing framework for studies of coordination problems in social service and health care delivery (Levine, White & Paul, 1963), technology transfer (Lambright & Teich, 1976), juvenile delinquency prevention (Miller, 1958), and court management (Dror, 1964), as well as investigations of federal support of local anti-poverty programs (Turk, 1973, 1970). Turk (1973: 37), in fact, has argued that "the study of complex urban phenomena is the study of organizations and their interrelations." Despite the widespread application of interorganizational theory, conceptual and methodological problems still exist in its use (Marrett, 1971; Schermerhorn, 1975). To clarify any conceptual confusion, the use of interorganizational theory and its relationship to urban intergovernmental cooperation are discussed below.

Schermerhorn (1975: 847) notes that interorganizational cooperation has been discussed in terms of "organizational interdependence, component interdependence, cooperation, exchange, and concerted decision making." An area of implied agreement in the literature is that cooperation among organizations is characterized by variance along some continuum. Warren's (1972) distinction among four decision-making contexts – social choice, coalition, federative, and unitary – provides some insight into the cooperation continuum. Within the social choice context, organizational interaction is unilaterally or mutually adaptive, but there is no concerting of decisions. The coalitional context is typified by voluntary cooperation on specific issues and little formal structure. In contrast to the coalitional context, the federative context is characterized by a formal interorganizational structure for a limited set of decisions and continuous, rather than ad hoc, interaction over these issues. Finally, "in the unitary context . . . organizational units are not autonomous but are part of a single hierarchical decision-making structure which orders their interaction, including the concerting of decisions" (Warren, 1972: 25).

Although Warren cautions that these constructs are ideal types, a partial mapping can be developed between Warren's constructs and forms of cooperation within urban information systems. For instance, the diffusion of technological innovations has frequently been described in terms of processes of social interaction (Rogers & Shoemaker, 1971; Rogers and Agarwala-Rogers, 1976). Organizations which respond to cues from other organizations or whose members interact with one another may, for example, decide unilaterally to adopt a particular computer application (Walker, 1969). A second, more formal, but voluntary form of cooperation occurs when computer applications are transferred. Application transfer involves one organization transmitting to another its documentation and probably temporary use of some of its personnel. The consolidated use of computing facilities, equipment, and personnel among local governments represents a form of cooperation corresponding to Warren's unitary context.

In addition to conceptualizing and defining urban intergovernmental cooperation in computing, it is useful to identify the phenomena of urban intergovernmental networks which are the focus of this analysis. Marrett (1971) identifies five foci of interorganizational analysis: 1) the intraorganizational properties of a given organization engaged in interaction; 2) comparison of the attributes of interacting organizations; 3) relational properties of interorganizational networks; 4) contextual analysis of the organizational and interorganizational environment in which interaction takes place; and 5) contextual analysis of social processes which affect interorganizational relations. The present study focuses primarily on the third through fifth levels of analysis. We are concerned with three questions in the context of computing technologies: 1) Are there relational or environmental properties of urban intergovernmental networks that speed the diffusion of technologies within the network?; 2) What characteristics of urban intergovernmental networks are associated with the level of transfer within the network?; 3) What relational or environmental properties of urban intergovernmental networks moderate or enhance the extent of cooperation among member units?

The final theoretical issue considered here is the nature of the antecedents of interorganizational cooperation. While the terminology used to describe the antecedents of interorganizational cooperation is quite heterogeneous, most researchers distinguish among three types of antecedents: need, opportunities, and the costs associated with cooperation (Schermerhorn, 1975). Need is a reflection of benefits potentially associated with interorganizational cooperation (Schermerhorn, 1975). Within this category of antecedents, both Turk and Schermerhorn distinguish between motivators that are objective reflections of need and those motivators that are subjective reflections of need, i.e., demand (Schermerhorn, 1975; Turk, 1973). Opportunities to cooperate consist of physical and normative factors which may influence the use of cooperation among the set of behavioral alternatives available to organizations (Schermerhorn, 1975; Turk, 1973). Need and opportunity are not sufficient by themselves to explain interorganizational cooperation but must be considered together with the costs associated with cooperation. The costs associated with cooperation are a function of distance among units within the network, the need for identity and autonomy of individual units, the existence of trade-off inducements or coercion, and the availability of slack resources (Schermerhorn, 1975; Turk, 1973; Warren, 1972).

CONCEPTUAL FRAMEWORK

The concepts discussed above are summarized in Fig. 6 (shown in italics). Need, opportunities, and associated costs are viewed as the major determinants of intergovernmental cooperation. These concepts are expected to influence the existence of various types of cooperation, the rate of diffusion, amount of transfer, and level of resource sharing among governmental units within an urban network.

To operationalize the concepts presented in Fig. 6, measures of the antecedent and outcome variables were constructed using data from the URBIS 1975 survey of local government computing in cities over 50,000 population and counties over 100,000 population and data from secondary sources (Appendix 1). For analytic purposes, Standard Metropolitan Statistical Areas (SMSAs) were then used to define the scope of the urban intergovernmental networks. Since the focus of the present study is upon networks of governmental units rather than individual or pairs of governmental units, only SMSAs for which data for three or more units were obtained were included in the analysis. Because only cities with populations greater than 50,000 and counties with populations greater than 100,000 were surveyed, smaller governmental units are excluded from the analysis. The exclusion of smaller governmental units could distort the results. However, prior to 1975, the use of computing by local governments was confined primarily to the cities and counties surveyed, so that the exclusion of smaller units should have no significant effect on the results.

Dependent Variables

We noted earlier that three types of information system cooperation can be identified within urban intergovernmental networks: diffusion, transfer, and resource sharing.

Because of the substantial number of computer applications currently being used by local governments, representative applications were chosen to measure the rate of diffusion, or overall spread of innovations. Revenue forecasting, budget preparation, police service data, and real property records were selected as applications that systematically differed on the rate and extent of diffusion.[1]

Transfer, or the movement of applications from one local government to another, was measured from survey responses of data processing personnel about the number of applications transferred to a city or county and the sources of these applications.

To measure the resource sharing variable, an index was created to reflect the extent to which each city or county in the SMSA used cooperative organizational arrangements in the delivery of data processing services. These arrangements could include the shared use of internal facilities, private

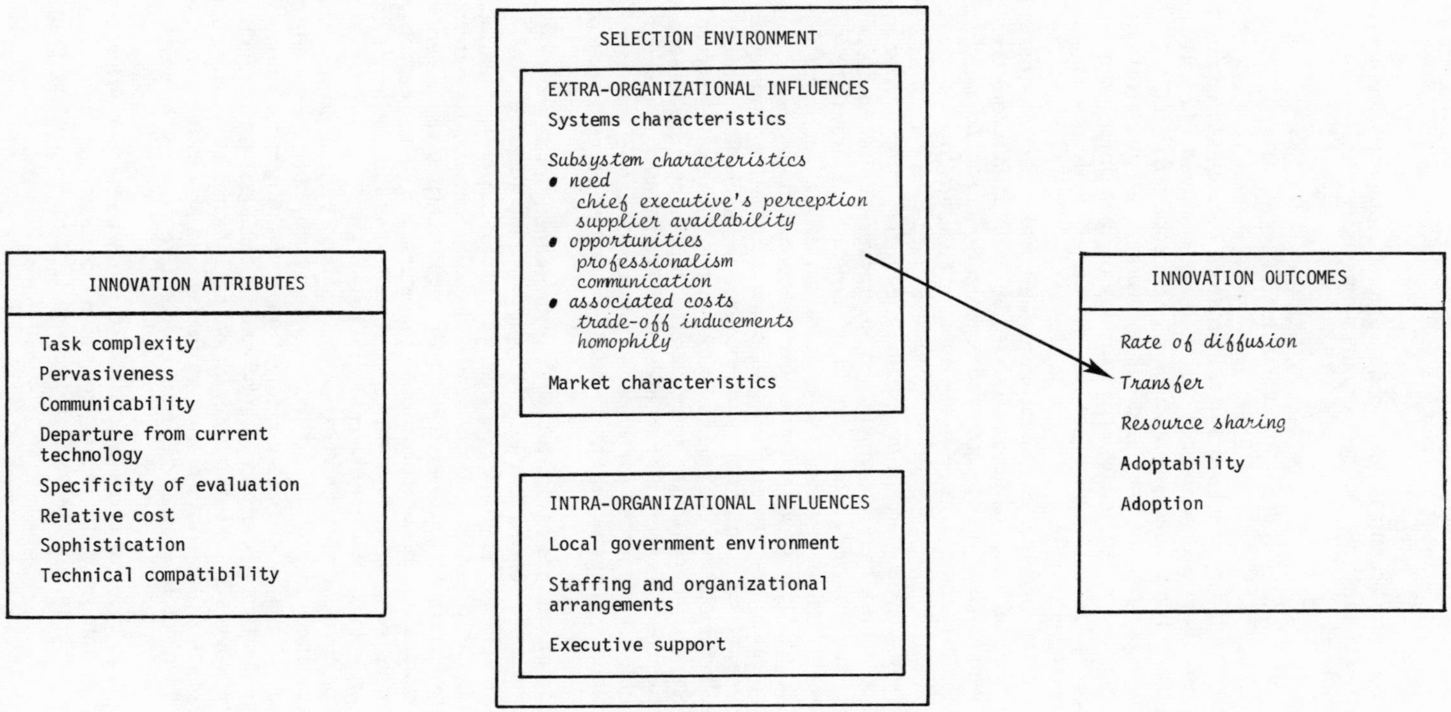

INNOVATION OUTCOMES

Rate of diffusion

Transfer

Resource sharing

Adoptability

Adoption

SELECTION ENVIRONMENT

EXTRA-ORGANIZATIONAL INFLUENCES

Systems characteristics

Subsystem characteristics
- *need*
  chief executive's perception
  supplier availability
- *opportunities*
  professionalism
  communication
- *associated costs*
  trade-off inducements
  homophily

Market characteristics

INTRA-ORGANIZATIONAL INFLUENCES

Local government environment

Staffing and organizational
arrangements

Executive support

INNOVATION ATTRIBUTES

Task complexity

Pervasiveness

Communicability

Departure from current
technology

Specificity of evaluation

Relative cost

Sophistication

Technical compatibility

Figure 6. EXPANSION OF THE SUBSYSTEMS CHARACTERISTICS COMPONENT OF THE ANALYTIC MODEL [a]

[a] The variables in italics represent the specific portion of the
analytic model examined in this chapter.

facilities management organizations, public regional computing centers, or some combination of these service delivery mechanisms.

Independent Variables

In developing the independent variables, indicators were classified into the three categories that we previously noted have received the greatest attention in the literature: need, opportunities, and associated costs.

Turk (1973) suggests that the need for interorganizational relations is derived from the awareness among organizations of their interdependence. Interdependence is, in turn, likely to be associated with a number of contextual characteristics.

Expenditure effort provides an indication of the fiscal capacity of network members. The need for cooperation is likely to be minimized where there is an adequate revenue base and no perceived organizational shortage of funds. Cooperation should become a more likely behavioral alternative as governmental units encounter increasingly restricted financial bases.

The chief executive's perception of the need for intergovernmental cooperation should also have an impact on intergovernmental interaction. City managers and mayors should be in a position to translate their perceptions into effective demands for cooperation as well as make other actors in their organizations aware of the need for cooperation.

Finally, the availability of computing supplies, information, and services may have an impact on interaction and cooperation. Schermerhorn (1975: 848) notes that "organizations may be favorably disposed toward interorganizational cooperation where there is a need to gain access to otherwise unavailable resources." In the absence of adequate suppliers of computing technology, local governments, particularly given restrictive competitive bidding requirements, may be willing to share resources or developmental costs.

A second set of factors associated with interorganizational cooperation are the opportunities to cooperate available to network members.

Schermerhorn (1975) suggests in this review of interorganizational cooperation that the prevailing norms of the organization and its external environment are significant influences upon the opportunities to cooperate. Both the professionalism of organizational members and the presence of supportive external communication networks should favorably influence the level of cooperation in urban intergovernmental networks.

Not only may environmental integration mechanisms such as professional associations influence interorganizational cooperation, but the level of intraorganizational integration among member units of the network may also be an important factor. Aiken and Hage's analysis (1968) of intraorganizational structure suggests that the integration of internal communication influences the organization's information gathering and processing potential and, thus, the level of interorganizational cooperative activity in which it engages.

Among the three types of cooperation, transfer may be further influenced by supplier programming. The extent to which hardware or commercial vendors provide programming services reflects a lack of internal programming capabilities and therefore the absence of resources necessary for transfer of applications. Furthermore, the extent of supplier programming represents a constraint on the transfer of a certain proportion of the local government's applications because of proprietary restrictions.

Our measurement of the associated costs of cooperation in urban networks is grounded in three concepts: the distance among governmental units within the network, the availability of trade-off inducements for cooperative ventures, and the availability of slack resources.

Rogers and Shoemaker (1971: 210) define homophily as "the degree to which pairs of individuals who interact are similar in certain attributes, such as beliefs, values, education, social status, and the like." Dominance-equivalence, social status differentials and wealth differentials are urban network analogs of the homophily concept, i.e., distance among units in the network. We would expect that the greater the distance or dissimilarity among units in the network, the less they will be inclined to engage in cooperative behavior.

Trade-off inducements represent another potential influence since they decrease the costs associated with certain activities. Thus, external funding, especially if requirements for cooperation are tied to reception of funding, increases the probability of cooperative activities.

Finally, the absence of slack resources has frequently been related in the literature to the propensity of actors to engage in transfer and resource sharing activities. Many proponents of computer application transfer and resource sharing suggest that benefits will be derived from more efficient utilization of resources.(2) Many of those who advocate transfer and resource sharing also argue that they are ideal means of capacity building with a minimum of resources. Thus, slack resources could be expected to be negatively related to transfer and resource sharing.

Operational definitions of these variables are presented in Appendix 2. The expected relationships between these measures and the dependent variables are presented in Table 7. Because diffusion can occur merely through information exchange and cue taking, and no formal resource sharing or coordination among organizations is necessary, the expected relationships between diffusion and the independent variables differs considerably from the expected relationships for transfer and resource sharing. Supplier activity, professionalism, environmental support, and trade-off inducements are expected to have significant associations with the variance of diffusion rates within urban intergovernmental networks. On the other hand, transfer and resource sharing are expected to be associated significantly with the associated cost variables, as well as with specific need and opportunity factors.

RESEARCH METHODOLOGY

Several steps were employed for testing and exploring the hypotheses set forth earlier. Given the definition of an urban intergovernmental network as an SMSA containing three or more governmental units with populations above the specified criteria, the number of cases included in these procedures was 54.

Table 7. EXPECTED RELATIONSHIPS BETWEEN DIFFUSION, TRANSFER, AND RESOURCE SHARING AND THE INDEPENDENT VARIABLES

	Diffusion	Transfer	Resource Sharing
NEED			
Revenue-Expenditure Effort			
Mean per capita general revenue	0	+	+
Mean per capita general expenditure	0	+	+
Perceived Need			
Chief executive perception of need for cooperation	0	+	+
Supplier Availability			
Mainframe sales offices	+	0	0
Product sales offices	+	0	0
Service sales offices	+	0	0
OPPORTUNITIES			
Professionalism	+	+	+
Environmental Support			
URISA members	+	+	+
URISA conference participation	+	+	+
Mean partisanship	-	-	-
Integration			
Interdepartmental data sharing	0	+	+
Supplier Programming			
Commercial programming mean	0	-	0
Hardware programming mean	0	-	0
ASSOCIATED COSTS			
Dominance-Equivalence			
Range of amount of intergovernmental revenue to units within the SMSA	0	-	-
Standard deviation of percent of SMSA population in each governmental unit	0	-	-
Economic-Wealth Differentials			
Range median school years completed among units within SMSA	0	-	-
Range of percent unemployed among units within the SMSA	0	-	-
Social Status Differentials			
Range within SMSA on community status scale	0	-	-
Range within SMSA on poverty scale	0	-	-
Trade-Off Inducements			
State funding	+	+	+
HUD 701 funding	+	+	+
LEAA funding	+	+	+
Revenue sharing funding	+	+	+
Slack Resources	0	-	-

First, bivariate correlations were computed between each of the independent and dependent variables. The bivariate correlations are presented in Table 8. Those independent variables which were correlated with one of the cooperation variables at or above the .10 level of significance were used in multiple regression analysis of each of the dependent variables. In several cases where similar independent variables were highly intercorrelated, for instance, the indicators of supplier activity, only one of the variables was entered into the regression. If two or more of the variables in the original regression had beta weights of at least one and half times their standard error, a second regression was run using just these variables. Finally, interaction terms were tested in several of the regressions. An interaction term, however, was significant only in the transfer regression.

RESEARCH FINDINGS

The regression results are reported in Table 9. Two general observations can be made on the basis of the predictions provided by the regression equations. The overall F-ratio is significant for each of the regression equations except for the rate of diffusion of the budget preparation application. On the other hand, a secondary summary indicator of the quality of the predictions, R^2, is generally low with the exception of the transfer equations.

Among the regressions for the rate of diffusion within urban intergovernmental networks, the significant independent variables are highly diverse. Only two variables are generally important across the application diffusion regressions: mainframe sales offices and LEAA funding. Since only one supplier activity variable was included in the regressions because of the higher intercorrelations among them, the significance of mainframe sales offices is an indication of the general importance of supplier activity in the rate of diffusion of applications within the intergovernmental network. The relationship between LEAA funding and the diffusion variables is less straightforward. As expected, LEAA funding is a positive and significant predictor of the diffusion rate for the police service data software application. However, it is negatively and significantly related to the diffusion of real property records applications and also negatively related to the diffusion of revenue forecasting and budget preparation applications.

Two other variables attain significant F-levels in the equations. Participation by individuals from the urban areas in URISA conferences had a significant effect on the intergovernmental diffusion of the revenue forecasting application. This suggests that professional associations may have some influence on the spread of urban technologies, but any influence, as indicated by the significance of URISA conference participation in only one case, is selective. Furthermore, it is interesting to note that participation and not merely membership is significantly associated with the diffusion rate for the revenue forecasting application. The other remaining variable to attain a significant F-level, mean partisanship, is negatively associated with the diffusion of budget preparation, police service data, and revenue forecasting applications.   It appears that partisanship within the urban network may generally retard the rapidity with which an application is widely accepted in a given geographic area.

Table 8. ZERO-ORDER CORRELATIONS BETWEEN THE INDEPENDENT VARIABLES AND DIFFUSION, TRANSFER AND RESOURCE SHARING

	Diffusion				Transfer	Resource Sharing
	Police Service Data	Real Property Records	Revenue Forecasting	Budget Preparation		
NEED						
Revenue-Expenditure Effort						
Mean per capita general revenue	.00	.09	.01	-.01	.02	.15
Mean per capita general expenditure	.08	.09	-.15	-.05	.09	.08
Perceived Need						
Chief executive perception of need for cooperation	.03	-.12	-.14	.04	.10	.05
Supplier Availability						
Mainframe sales offices	.29**	.10	.29**	.19	-.06	-.01
Product sales offices	.21*	.11	.20	.15	.00	-.04
Service sales offices	.17	.06	.20	.14	.01	-.06
OPPORTUNITIES						
Professionalism						
Legislative support and management objectives	.05	-.03	.25**	.05	-.13	-.02
Use of objectives and performance criteria	.15	-.17	.23*	.05	-.19	-.16
Environmental Support						
URISA members	.14	-.09	.35***	.11	.07	-.29**
URISA conference participation	.13	-.13	.41***	.14	.05	-.25**
Mean partisanship	-.26**	.12	-.27**	-.36***	-.12	.16
Integration						
Interdepartmental data sharing	-.06	.07	.01	.14	.29	.10
Supplier Programming						
Commercial programming mean	-.10	-.16	-.05	-.23*	-.17	-.11
Hardware programming mean	-.17	-.18	-.16	-.38***	-.18	-.11
ASSOCIATED COSTS						
Dominance-Equivalence						
Range of amount of intergovernmental revenue to units within the SMSA	.21*	.13	.05	.11	-.06	-.05
Standard deviation of percent of SMSA population in each governmental unit	-.19	-.22*	.11	.08	.03	-.20
Economic-Wealth Differentials						
Range median school years completed among units within the SMSA	-.19	.04	-.05	.03	-.06	-.16
Range of percent unemployed among units within the SMSA	-.13	.08	.03	.02	-.07	-.15
Special Status Differentials						
Range on community status scale	.28**	.05	.22*	.10	-.07	.07
Range within SMSA on poverty scale	.23**	.12	.16	.06	.06	.04
Trade-off Inducements						
State funding	-.10	.15	-.13	.02	-.04	.04
HUD 701 funding	-.10	-.21	.15	-.01	-.10	-.13
LEA funding	-.27**	-.23**	-.18	-.17	.02	-.05
Revenue sharing funding	-.27**	-.25**	-.14	-.03	.50***	-.05
Slack Resources	.00	.05	.00	.18	.66***	-.03

*p < .05
**p < .025
***p < .01

Table 9. MULTIPLE REGRESSION RESULTS FOR RATE OF DIFFUSION, TRANSFER AND RESOURCE SHARING IN URBAN INTERGOVERNMENTAL NETWORKS

Dependent Variables / Independent Variables	Mainframe sales offices	Professional management orientation	URISA members	URISA conference participation	Partisanship mean	Interdepartmental data sharing	Hardware vendor programming mean	Range of % inter-governmental revenues	Standard deviation of % SMSA population in each city	SMSA range on community status scale	HUD funding	LEAA funding	Revenue sharing funding	Slack resources	Slack resources X revenue sharing funding	Constant	R^2	F
RATE OF DIFFUSION																		
Police service data	.15				-.25			.15				.32**				17.60	.19	2.80*
Real property records		.23					.07		-.14		-.25	-.26*	-.24			16.20	.23	2.85*
		.21									-.25	-.25*	-.28*			14.88	.18	3.91*
Revenue forecasting	.18			.25	-.16					-.03		-.11				-8.53	.26	2.79**
	.16			.33**												-18.68	.22	4.83***
Budget preparation	.13				-.20		-.20					-.24		.15		26.90	.17	1.89
					-.30*		-.17					-.16				34.05	.15	2.88*
TRANSFER		-.13				-.12	-.20						.34***	.63***		.15	.63	14.88***
							-.16						.38***	.57***	.52***	.05	.60	24.61***
							-.10						.30***	.15		.04	.65	24.63***
RESOURCE SHARING			-.31**						-.09							1.13	.11	3.40*

* p .05
** p .025
*** p .01

The transfer of applications within urban intergovernmental networks is associated with variables distinguishable from those important in predicting diffusion. Three variables account for a significant portion of the variance in transfers: the mean for hardware vendor programming of applications, the mean of revenue sharing funding, and the mean level of slack resources among the governmental units.

Although no conclusions about causal relationships can be drawn from the transfer results, several interesting relationships are suggested. Employing hardware vendors to program applications could reflect reduced opportunities for transfers within urban intergovernmental networks, since hardware vendor programming indicates a substitute means for incorporating data processing applications. Alternatively, the relationship between outside vendor programming and transfer could be attributable to difficulties associated with transferring vendor programmed applications to other local government contexts. It is extremely plausible that in order to maintain their markets, external suppliers would design software for local governments so that transfer is difficult.

The fact that both revenue sharing funding and slack resources are positively and significantly associated with transfer in intergovernmental networks suggests the need for the availability of considerable resource flexibility before transfers can occur. This finding, coupled with the fact that none of the need variables are significantly related to transfer, indicates a severe weakness in the current arguments of proponents of transfer. Proponents suggest that transfer is an economical means of developing applications software, especially for organizations which lack substantial resources for software development. However, these findings imply that urban intergovernmental transfer increases with the availability of slack resources. The significant increase in the multiple R when a revenue sharing-slack resources multiplicative term is added supports this line of reasoning. The change in the multiple R when the multiplicative term is included in the regression produces an F of 5.35 which is significant at the .025 level.

The lowest R^2 achieved by the regression equations is that for resource sharing. Only two zero-order correlations, URISA membership, and the standard deviation of percent SMSA population in each city, were signifcant at the .10 level or better. When these variables are entered into the regression, only URISA is statistically significant and, contrary to expectations, in a negative direction. Again, although causality cannot be inferred from this relationship, one causal interpretation is highly plausible. Low concentrations of professionals among governmental units within an urban network serves as a centripetal force, motivating resource pooling among local governments. In contrast, substantial concentrations of professionals would have a greater interest in the autonomy of their organization's computing resources, thus creating a centrifugal force within the network.

DISCUSSION

With respect to interorganizational theory, the results suggest that the use of interorganizational analysis may well be fruitful in social choice and coalitional contexts. However, in federative contexts, i.e., full-fledged cooperative efforts, the use of interorganizational theory was much less fruitful. The results suggest that the explanatory and predictive power of interorganizational theory may be limited to situations where organizations maintain significant levels of autonomy.

Several practical implications may also be drawn from these results. First, the diffusion and transfer results suggest that, because of both the diversity and nature of the factors associated with these innovation outcomes, we may expect very uneven success records from demonstration programs for urban management technologies. Since the correlates of diffusion rates within urban intergovernmental networks for different applications are highly diverse, demonstration programs which fail to recognize this diversity are unlikely to be generally successful. Similarly, demonstration programs designed for technology transfer must recognize the role of "slack" in facilitating transfer. Diffusion and transfer strategies must therefore consider these factors to develop more flexible and appropriate programs.

Second, the anomalies for the federal funding variables suggest that policymakers may need to consider the unintended consequences of support for some applications but not for others. The heavy promotion of new development in one area tends to slow down or to retard development in other areas. This might occur because local government computing capacity is fixed at any point in time and can be changed only in large increments over a long time period. Most local governments assume that federal support is transitory and therefore shift development priorities temporarily rather than increase capacity. This tends to displace other planned development and, thus, changes the pattern of local applications.

CONCLUSION

Characteristics of the urban intergovernmental network which were significant in explaining the rate of diffusion of computer applications were highly diverse across the applications considered in the analysis. Depending on the applications, the activity of suppliers within the network, organizational professionalism, and the level of outside funding may have positive or negative associations with the variance in the rate of diffusion.

The transfer of applications within intergovernmental networks was associated with variables distinguishable from those important in predicting diffusion. Although the results are only suggestive, the findings indicate that vendor programming of applications and high concentrations of professionals exert negative influences on resource sharing, while the availability of flexible resources and low concentrations of professionals may exert positive influences on resource sharing.

3 The Influence of Market Variables*

In this chapter we look at market characteristics and application attributes that may influence the physical transfer of computer applications between local governments. Data on market characteristics (locus of the developer, geographic proximity and similarity of transfer sites, sophistication of the transferees, and the adopter's past transfer experience) and innovation attributes (sophistication of applications and technical compatibility) are used to evaluate a number of widely held beliefs about the transfer of computer applications. The results of the evaluation are used to draw several conclusions about the nature of the application transfer market in local governments.

Transfer refers to the process of moving an innovation developed in one local government to another local government. Generally, computer application transfer is referred to as a process of moving a computer application developed at a high cost in one place to another place at a lower cost than would be required to develop the application locally. It has been widely acclaimed as a means by which local governments can achieve substantial cost savings and increased efficiency. The appeal of the computer application transfer is considerable and stems from four common beliefs:

---

*Portions of this chapter appeared in Kenneth L. Kraemer, "Local Government, Information Systems, and Technology Transfer: Evaluating Some Common Assertions About Computer Application Transfer," Public Administration Review, Vol. 37 (July/August 1977), pp. 368-382. They are reprinted by permission of the American Society for Public Administration.

- Transfer capitalizes on the portability of applications.

- Transfer saves time and money for the transferee.

- Transfer quickly upgrades the computing sophistication of transferees.

- Transfer involves only minor technical problems to be overcome.

Transfer capitalizes on the portability of applications

Computer applications, like other technologies, are seen as interchangeable from one site to another having plug-in features in the sense that they are relatively self-contained, prepackaged and readily learnable, and their implementation can be buffered against the impact of the larger environment; through rudimentary training of the transferees, the applications can be brought in and made operational, thereby preventing continual "reinvention of the wheel."(1) The sophistication of the application particularly affects the transferability of applications among local governments.

Transfer saves time and money for the transferee

Since computer applications are self-contained and portable, they can be moved without regard to the compatibility of host computers, and they can be moved to a new site much more quickly and cheaply than they can be built at the new site. Thus, only one site need bear development costs, and all others need pay only for transfer and implementation expenses. The greater the sophistication of the applications the greater the marginal cost for development, and therefore the greater the potential savings from applications transfer.

Transfer quickly upgrades the computing sophistication of transferees

Normally, high costs and long development periods are associated with evolving computing sophistication in local governments. With inexpensive and rapid transfer of computer applications, it is possible for sites with low levels of computing sophistication to quickly modernize. The less the sophistication of the transferee the greater the potential benefits from transfer. This belief is often cited as an argument for more extensive transfer from technologically sophisticated local governments to those still developing technological skills. Thus, the adoptor's past transfer experience is not expected to affect future transfers.

Transfer involves only minor technical problems to be overcome

Since applications are self-contained and portable, the primary difficulties faced in transfer are technical shortfalls such as lack of standardization. This is particularly true where the transfer occurs between organizations with similar functions and goals. The locus of the developer, the similarity of transfer governments, and the proximity of transfer sites are immaterial to application transfer.

CONCEPTUAL FRAMEWORK

These four beliefs cover most of the arguments in support of computer application transfer. Implicit in these beliefs are hypotheses about the current and future scope of transfer activity, its relations to the attributes of computer applications, and its relations to the characteristics of the local government transfer market. These hypotheses, which are discussed below, are incorporated in the conceptual model for this analysis (shown in italics in Fig. 7). If they prove to be sound, then transfer can be considered the ideal mechanism for spreading the benefits of computer technology.

The major hypotheses are as follows. With regard to the scope of transfer activity, current transfer of applications among local governments should be extensive because of the potential benefits it offers. But, since transfer of computer applications is a comparatively new practice, and just catching on, current transfer figures might not entirely reflect the number of governments interested in transfer. At a minimum, however, transfers of applications should equal in-house development of applications, and those sites without past transfer experience should at least be planning to transfer applications.

With regard to specific transfer decisions, certain innovation attributes should influence what applications are selected for transfer. Because computer applications are highly portable and technical problems in transfer are minimal, the computer applications transferred should not show any tendency towards technical compatibility of host computers. Also, since local governments are concerned with minimizing costs, the computer applications transferred should tend to be those with the highest marginal cost for development – in other words, the more complex and sophisticated applications that would cost a great deal to develop in-house.

Concern with cost effectiveness should also result in varying impacts of market variables on specific transfer decisions. Transfer of computer applications should tend to take place from the more sophisticated sites to less sophisticated sites, and from the sites with transfer experience to sites without such experience. However, transfer of computer applications should not be influenced by the similarity of the transfer governments, the geographic proximity of the transfer sites, or the locus of the developer due to the ease with which software is moved.

The measures used for testing the relationships among the variables in these hypotheses are explained next.

Dependent Variables

The scope of transfer was measured by responses concerning the number of applications transferred within the past two years and the number of applications planned for transfer within the next two years.

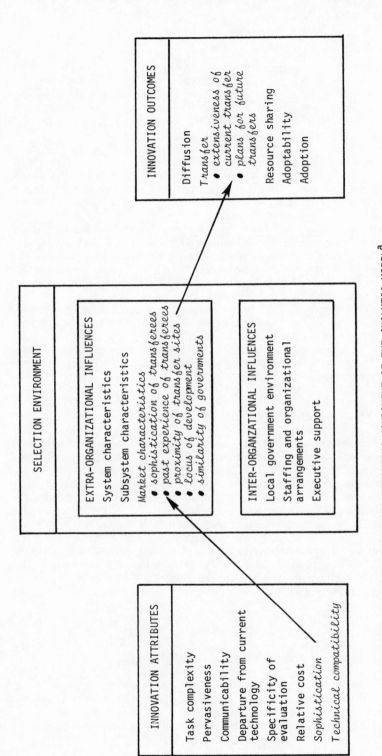

Figure 7. EXPANSION OF THE MARKET CHARACTERISTICS COMPONENT OF THE ANALYTIC MODEL[a]

---

[a] The variables in italics represent the specific portion of the analytic model examined in this chapter.

Independent Variables

The sophistication of applications transferred was measured by responses concerning the kinds of applications transferred. Management oriented applications such as budget monitoring, fire incident reporting, and fire station locator were classified as more sophisticated, while operations oriented applications such as payroll preparation, general accounting, and utility billing were classified as less sophisticated.

The technical compatibility of host computers was measured by responses indicating whether the application was transferred from one host computer mainframe to another host computer mainframe with the same or different characteristics.

The sophistication of the transferring governments was measured by data drawn from the survey concerning population size, electronic data processing (EDP) expenditures, computer core capacity, and operational applications.

The similarity of governments involved in transfer was measured by whether the transfer was between two governments of the same type (city to city) or of different types (city to county).

The proximity of transfer sites was measured by responses as to whether applications were transferred from within the state, between adjacent states, within the region, or across regions.

The locus of development was measured by whether the applications were transferred from one local government to another local government, or from a federal or state source to a local government.

RESEARCH METHODOLOGY

Primarily descriptive statistics were used in this analysis. The data used in the analysis were drawn from a portion of the URBIS project Application Questionnaires specifically dealing with past transfers and plans for transfer(2), and from a portion of the Installation Questionnaire dealing with computing equipment, EDP budgets, and computer applications (Appendix 1). Of the 381 cities and 288 counties (N=669) responding to the URBIS survey, 65 percent responded to the transfer experience portion of the survey. Of these, approximately 22 percent or 100 governments had transfer experience; 51 were cities and 49 were counties and they had transferred 149 applications between them. Sixty percent of the URBIS cities responded to the transfer plans portion of the survey. Of these, approximately 23 percent or 91 governments had transfer plans; 54 were cities and 37 were counties.

RESEARCH FINDINGS

Present and Future Scope of Transfer

Transfer of computer applications is much less common than in-house development. In fact, as shown in Table 10, only 23 percent of the governments surveyed had transferred applications within the past two years. This contrasts with 66 percent of the governments having developed in-house applications over the past two years. Additionally, the average number of transferred applications per site (1.5) is not nearly as large as the average number of applications per site developed in-house (5.8).

Contrary to the hypothesis, there is no substantial planned transfer of applications among the governments surveyed. Table 11 shows that only 23 percent of the local governments plan transfers within the next two years. This contrasts with 85 percent of the governments planning in-house development of applications within the next two years. And, the average number of planned transfers per site (1.3) is much lower than the average number of in-house applications planned for the next two years (25.1). Even granting the argument that the relative newness of transfer has resulted in few current transfers, the data indicate that there will be little growth in transfers over the next two years. Moreover, Table 12 indicates there is little increase in the total number of sites that will have transferred in the next two years. Nearly two-thirds of the sites planning transfer have already been involved in transfer.

Transfer Market Influences

Rather than transfers occurring from more sophisticated to less sophisticated sites, and from experienced to inexperienced sites, as the hypothesis

Table 10.   EXTENSIVENESS OF APPLICATION TRANSFER AMONG SURVEYED LOCAL GOVERNMENTS[a]

	Cities	Counties	Totals
Percentage of local governments with transfer experience over the last 2 years	18%	29%	23%
Average number of applications transferred per transfer site	1.4	1.6	1.5
Percentage of local governments engaging in in-house application development over the last 2 years	65%	67%	66%
Average number of applications developed in-house per development site	6.3	5.4	5.8

[a]Of the 669 respondents, 65% answered survey questions on transfer and in-house development experiences.

predicts, transfer takes place primarily among sophisticated and experienced sites. Tables 13 and 14 show that transfer has occurred most among larger local governments, and that these transfer governments tend to have higher expenditures for data processing, larger computers, more operational applications, more on-line applications, and more applications documented. And Table 13 also shows that two-thirds of the sites planning transfer have already been involved in transfer. Taken together, these measures indicate a comparatively high level of computing sophistication and prior transfer experience among transfer sites.

Table 15 shows that transfer is highly related to the similarity and geographic proximity of governments, contrary to the hypothesis. Most transfers (73 percent) were between similar governments (Table 15). Thirty-nine percent of the transfers were from one county to another county and 34 percent were from one city to another city. Mixed transfers (city to county or county to city) accounted for only 27 percent of the total. Most transfers also were between geographically proximate governments. Sixty-four percent were between governments in the same state and another 15 percent between governments in adjacent states whereas only 21 percent were between governments within the same region or across regions. However, cities and counties show an interesting difference in the geographic proximity of transfer sites. Most county-to-county transfers (86%) were within the same state; only 4 percent were across regions or within regions. In contrast, only one-third of the city-to-city transfers were within the same state; 45 percent were across regions or within regions. Thus, while geographic proximity clearly is important for transfer by both cities and counties, it appears to be more important to counties than to cities.

Table 11.   PLANS FOR COMPUTER APPLICATIONS TRANSFER AMONG SURVEYED LOCAL GOVERNMENTS[a]

	Cities	Counties	Totals
Percentage of local governments planning applications transfer	22%	25%	23%
Average number of planned transfers per transfer site	1.1	1.6	1.3
Percentage of local governments planning in-house development	87%	83%	85%
Average number of planned in-house applications developments per site	28	23	25

[a]Of the 669 respondents, 60% answered survey questions on transfer and in-house development plans.

THE INFLUENCE OF MARKET VARIABLES   59

Table 12.   OVERLAP OF LOCAL GOVERNMENTS THAT HAVE TRANSFERRED AND PLAN
             TO TRANSFER COMPUTER APPLICATIONS[a]

| | | Have Transferred | | |
		Yes	No	Total
	Yes	60	31	91
Plan to Transfer	No	40	305	345
	Total	100	336	436

[a] $\left[x^2 = 120.3 > 10.8 = x^2 \ .001^{(df\ =\ 1)} \right]$

Also contrary to the hypothesis, Table 16 indicates that the preponderance of transfers occur between local governments themselves (87%), while a much smaller fraction (13%) occur from transfer centers such as the federal or state governments, or urban technology transfer agencies. Apparently, there is some advantage in being both proximate and similar to a site from which one is transferring an application, a condition that indicates transfers require substantial communication between transferor and transferee.

Table 13.   A BREAKDOWN OF LOCAL GOVERNMENTS TRANSFERRING COMPUTER APPLICATIONS, BY POPULATION*

TRANSFER EXPERIENCE

Categories	Cities		Counties	
	URBIS Respondents (A)	Have transferred in last two years (% of A)	URBIS Respondents (B)	Have transferred in last two years (% of B)
Totals	284	18%	171	29%
Population Groups				
500,000 and over	19	42	38	34
250,000 - 499,999	27	22	38	34
100,000 - 249,999	74	15	87	26
50,000 - 99,999	164	16	--	--

TRANSFER PLANS

Categories	Cities		Counties	
	URBIS Respondents (A)	Have transferred in last two years (% of A)	URBIS Respondents (B)	Have transferred in last two years (% of B)
Totals	250	22%	151	25%
Population Groups				
500,000 and over	15	27	32	25
250,000 - 499,999	23	30	41	22
100,000 - 249,999	66	23	78	26
50,000 - 99,999	146	19	--	--

* 119 cities and 139 counties failed to answer this question.

Table 14.   COMPARATIVE TECHNICAL SOPHISTICATION AMONG LOCAL GOVERNMENTS
THAT HAVE TRANSFERRED APPLICATIONS

Indicators of EDP Development Status	Cities		Counties	
	Transfer Sites	All URBIS Cities	Transfer Sites	All URBIS Counties
Average EDP expenditures	$948,384	$572,210	$861,883	$487,000
Average EDP expenditures as a % of total operating budget	1.6%	1.0%	1.7%	1.3%
Average total core capacity in bytes	515K	165K	470K	338K
Average total operational applications	39	28	39	30
Average total operational applications on-line	12	6	6	5
Average total operational applications with documentation	25	16	26	19

Influences of Application Attributes

Contrary to the hypothesis that technical compatibility is unimportant in transfer, Table 17 indicates that most transfers occur between cities with highly compatible host computers for the transferred application. Seventy-two percent of the transfers involved at least the same manufacturer. Of these, 55 percent involved either the same computer or the same model; another 17 percent involved different models of the same manufacturer (Table 17). Only 28 percent of the transfers involved different computer manufacturers as the host for the transferred application.

Also contrary to the hypothesis, those applications that are more sophisticated tend not to be the applications most transferred. Instead, as shown in Tables 18 and 19, the relatively few applications that are transferred tend to be simple and operations-oriented. If transfer is as easy and cost-saving as predicted, one would expect more transfers of very expensive and complex applications where the potential savings would be greatest; yet, this is not the case.

Table 15. SIMILARITY AND PROXIMITY OF TRANSFER SITES (N=113)

Similarity of Governments Involved in Transfers	Percent of transfers which are:				
	Within State	Between Adjacent States	Within Regions	Across Regions	Total
City to city (34%)	34%	21%	16%	29%	100%
County to county (39%)	87	9	2	2	100
County to city (10%)	73	18	0	9	100
City to county (18%)	65	15	15	5	100
Total (100%)					

Table 16. SOURCE OF TRANSFERRED APPLICATIONS

Transferred from:	Cities		Counties		Totals	
SOURCE OF TRANSFERRED APPLICATIONS						
Local to Local[a]	78%	(54)	95%	(76)	87%	(130)
Federal/State to Local[b]	22	(15)	5	(4)	13	(19)
Totals	100	(69)	100	(80)	100	(149)

[a]From either a city or county to another city or county

[b]From a federal or state agency or an urban technology transfer agency

Clearly, all of the hypotheses are shown to be inconsistent with the data. This indicates that common beliefs about transfer may belie the realities of actual experience.

DISCUSSION

The foregoing results suggest that computer application transfer might have less appeal than predicted by its promoters. This is probably because the benefits from transfer are less and the costs greater than proponents acknowledge. Apparently, transfer is much more problematic than it first appears. Why is this the case? How do the four beliefs about application transfer differ from the realities of transfer experience and the associations among the variables we have just explored? We re-examine here each of the four beliefs reflecting on problems with each.

Table 17. TECHNICAL COMPATIBILITY OF HOST COMPUTERS OF TRANSFERRED APPLICATIONS[a]

Transferred Applications ran on:	Number of Transfers	Percent
Same manufacturer, same computer (e.g., IBM 370/145 to IBM 370/145)	26	31%
Same manufacturer, same model (e.g., IBM 370/145 to IBM 370/158)	20	24
Same manufacturer, different mainframe (e.g., IBM 360 to IBM 370)	14	17
Different manufacturers (e.g., IBM and NCR)	24	28
	84[b]	100

[a] The ease of transfer is based on the compatibility of the host computer mainframes in the transfer sites. Generally, transfer is easier when it involves the same computer in both sites than when it involves two different computers.

[b] For 16 of the transfer sites, it was not possible to identify one of the computers in the transfer dual because of missing data.

Transfer Capitalizes on the "Portability" of Applications

Computer applications are often less portable than they appear. All applications of computing include much more than physical hardware and software. These technologies are used in social settings, complete with all the complexity and vagueness associated with people and their interactions. Local conditions of the transferee can differ greatly from those of the transferor. Local operating procedures may be different. Local values may be different. Even physical conditions can differ from place to place.

The data clearly showed that most transfers are between similar governments and geographically proximate governments. This is primarily due to the importance of differences in local procedures for doing various tasks that exist between sites. This is especially true with respect to county governments, and to a lesser extent with respect to cities, since counties perform many functions delegated by the states and each state has its own laws governing the practices of its cities and counties. A financial management system or welfare system built for a California county, for example, seldom works for a county in the state of Washington without extensive modification. The conflict that arises in such situations is obvious: either the local conditions must be changed to accommodate the technology, or the technology must be modified to fit the local conditions. In the majority of cases, the technology must be modified or abandoned.

Another problem in application transfer occurs with transferors or donor sites, especially when these donor sites are not in the business of developing applications for transfer. The first few occasions in which a donor assists a transferee with information, documentation and advice may represent an acceptable cost for the donor in terms of professional prestige by being considered "technologically advanced." But as demands for transfer assistance increase, a donor can soon be swamped with costs for assisting others. The donor is then faced with two choices: cease assisting in transfer efforts, or begin charging for services. The former effectively eliminates transfer; the latter entails going into business that may not coincide with the major

Table 18.   SOPHISTICATION OF APPLICATIONS TRANSFERRED

Sophistication of Application	Cities	Counties	Total
Management-oriented	25	18	43
Operations-oriented	44	62	106
Totals	69	80	149

Table 19.   ILLUSTRATIVE APPLICATIONS TRANSFERRED[a]

Function	Number Transferred
Law enforcement statistics/Crime reporting	4
Law enforcement "package"	3
Fire incident reporting	4
Fire station locator	3
Jury selection	7
General accounting	11
Payroll preparation and accounting	12
Budget monitoring	2
Budget preparation/Accounting	6
Water/Electric billing	3
Assistance records/Food stamps/Disabled/general	8
Information and referral	3
Catalogue/Circulation	3
Registration records	3
Vote counting	3

[a]This table presents only applications categories showing two or more transfers. This accounts for 75 out of 149 reported transfers. The remainder of transfers reported were single examples spread over more than 200 possibilities.

objectives of the donor organization. This is particularly true with respect to urban governments that often have enough trouble dealing with the tasks before them.(3)

Aside from the difficulties associated with actually moving applications from one site to another, most transfer arguments overlook the tremendous benefits that can accrue from "re-inventing the wheel." The biggest benefit that local governments can reap from in-house development of technologies is learning. And, they learn about the technology with a much greater depth than is possible under transfer circumstances. This is particularly true when one considers that a great deal of learning occurs in trying to overcome difficulties, often the very difficulties that transfer is supposed to avoid. Transfer efforts often exceed the ability of the transferee to accommodate the technology effectively, and deprive the transferee of the learning experiences that come with developing more slowly and methodically.

Transfer saves Time and Money for the Transferee

Assuming that a transfer takes place with ideal "plug-to-plug" precision and requires little modification, time and money can be saved. However, costs of transfer go up very quickly when modifications commence. Not only must time be spent making the modifications themselves, but time also must be spent by local talent learning the transferred system in detail so that the changes are made properly. Further, several major problems which increase costs can emerge when trying to move applications from one site to another.

The host computing environments for the transferred applications are incompatible. The great variety in computer mainframes, operating systems, data base management systems, and peripheral devices used among local governments creates compatibility problems in adopting applications from one computing environment to another. The variety in mainframes and operating systems is not only due to the variety of makes and models available, but also due to the many changes that occur over time to the mainframes and operating systems. In addition, the applications themselves evolve through enhancements. Thus, for a particular computer application to be transferable, it must exist in multiple versions, and "version control" becomes a major problem in itself.

The application is poorly documented. Proper documentation is essential to transfer of any computer application. Without clear and comprehensive written descriptions and instructions, it is very difficult for a transferee to adequately judge the merits of an application before adopting it for transfer, or to adapt and install any application adopted. Many governments have had the unfortunate experience of finding a problem in a transferred application that was not documented, and that rendered the application almost useless in the transfer site.

The application is poorly designed to begin with. This problem can be serious, but often is less obvious to transferees than it should be. Transferees frequently are unable to discriminate between a well-designed or poorly-designed application which requires extensive modification to do an adequate job. For example, one city transferred in a computerized accounting package from another city only to find after installation that it contained very poor audit trails. In order to modify the system sufficiently to satisfy state law, the transferee had to redevelop the program at considerable additional cost.

The application is not designed for transfer. Most efforts at application transfer take existing computer applications, developed without the special problems of transfer in mind, and move them directly to a transferee. Thus, even simple design features that facilitate transfer, such as standardized nomenclature in documentation, may be overlooked. The costs of overcoming such inadequacies in the design may be considerable.

The application is part of a larger, integrated information system. Thus, the transferred application may either exceed transferee requirements or it may be handicapped in operation unless used in conjunction with the integrated system. The first of these cases can be seen in this quote from an observer of the USAC Project (Hemmens, 1975, p. 19):

> Remember that in taking an IMIS (Integrated Municipal Information System) product that you are taking a part of a larger system, but that system doesn't exist (in your situation). So there may well be programming niceties, data handling, and so forth that are unnecessary and turn out to be costs rather than benefits.

An example of the second problem — the need for an integrated system in order to reap the benefits of the transferred system — can be seen in the case of computerized criminal records systems that depend on large, integrated networks to supply the data necessary to make them useful to local sites.

Transfer Facilitates Modernization of Low-sophistication Sites

The data on computer applications clearly show that most transfers occur between sites with considerable sophistication rather than from sophisticated to unsophisticated sites. This occurs for several reasons. First, transfer is dependent on extensive professional contacts among transfer sites. Larger, more sophisticated sites have a greater opportunity to engage in extensive professional sharing and, indeed, often have their own organizations that exclude smaller, less-sophisticated members.(4) It is only through these contacts that transferable applications are found, and the promotional claims about applications investigated sufficiently to encourage moving ahead with a transfer.

Second, transferees require considerable in-house experience to evaluate the feasibility and value of a potential transfer. There are many issues to be investigated before undertaking a transfer: will the transfer technology adapt to existing local technology; will it require modification to fit local customs and procedures; will users be satisfied with the new technology and use it; will the cost of modifications to the technology eliminate the cost savings from transfer? Dealing successfully with these crucial concerns requires a detailed understanding of both the local site and the transfer technology. Most larger, sophisticated sites have such capability, but few small, unsophisticated sites do.

Third, assuming a technology is adopted for transfer, it requires local expertise to install the technology, make it operational, train the users, and keep the local technologies working during adaptation. This kind of expertise can usually be bought from the transferor or from a transfer agent. But, the cost may be very high and the transferee loses the opportunity to develop in-house capability.

Therefore, transfer probably is inappropriate as a quick means of upgrading low sophistication sites. It might be possible to accelerate development toward higher sophistication, but at a pace that can be accommodated by the local site.

Technological Shortfalls are the Primary Cause of Transfer Failures

Technical impediments clearly can create increased costs in transfer, and even abort transfer efforts.(5) However, technical impediments to moving many kinds of urban technology have declined markedly in the past few years, particularly within national boundaries. In the field of local government computing, for example, a large set of standards for computing operations has been informally accepted and is now common. Also, the majority of local governments use equipment manufactured by IBM, and do their computer programming in COBOL or FORTRAN languages. Most compatibility problems have known solutions, so they can be overcome given time and money.

Considerable resistance to transfer might develop among local technical personnel, as the prospect of having to work with others' technical creations is often less exciting than building their own creations in-house. Design is the sine qua non of technical professions such as engineering and computer programming, and transfer can supplant this creative, satisfying activity with tedious "debugging" work. Further, many designers prefer to work with "leading edge" technology rather than within the mainstream of existing urban technology. It is more prestigious, and generally more fun, to design technologies that are fancier than normal.(6) However, these technologies rarely can be transferred to many other places.

Users, similarly, often take pride in the small differences between the way they do their tasks and the way their counterparts in other locations do theirs. This pride in small differences is part of building and maintaining an image of professional superiority over their counterparts. Thus, many users might be unwilling to accept technologies built to conform to the practices and standards of their counterparts in other places, feeling that they can do a better job by building their own technology. Both of these kinds of resistance are common in cases where application transfer is attempted among sites with comparable technical capability.

Resistance to transfer also might come from bureaucratic incentives and resource politics in urban governments. When an application is developed in-house the resources of the local site go to increase total capability. Transfer, however, usually results in resources being given to the transferor or to the transfer agent. The net effect is that the local site loses an opportunity to build up its budgetary status, and must often use its "slack resources" to deal with unanticipated costs of transfer. These erosions of potential funds might be acceptable to managers if they were rewarded for efficient resource use, but, unfortunately, there is no more professional prestige from transfer for managers than there is for technical personnel and users. Since most bureaucratic agencies follow a "budgeting-from-past-history" practice, managers are generally rewarded with increased budgets only for accumulating in-house staff, and for using their staff less efficiently than possible (Crecine, 1967; 1969).

Lastly, few institutional incentives exist for generalized technological development among the donor sites.(7) In the case of a donor site that simply builds technology for its own use, a generalized design costs more and fulfills local needs less well than a tailored design. Among donor sites that wish to sell their technologies, a generalized design might be unattractive to the organizations that make up their market. Thus, most urban technologies are designed suboptimally for local conditions, making them difficult to transfer. Clearly, then, a combination of suboptimal specifications, "leading edge" design features, and local resistance to outside technology might seriously impede successful transfer. These institutional and behavioral problems are at least as serious as technical factors in transfer failures, and frequently more so.

CONCLUSION

The model we set up in this chapter was based primarily on relationships implicit in the beliefs of proponents of transfer as a method of technological diffusion. Associated with the arguments of the proponents is the explicit notion that local governments can achieve substantial savings and increased efficiency by transferring costly computer applications developed at one local government to another local government.

Our analysis indicates that relations among variables implicit in the arguments of those who state the case for technology transfer are not supported by empirical analysis. These findings coincide with the overall finding that technology transfer is much less extensive than could be expected based on the overall cost-benefit argument. Underlying this finding are several technical, behavioral, and institutional barriers which contribute to the overall cost of transfer, and also reduce its benefits. Consequently, although application transfer may be a good idea, the realities of implementation currently make the concept problematic.

II

Adoption of Computer Applications by Local Governments

4 Environmental Determinants*

The first of our micro level analyses investigates the characteristics of the local government organization and its environment that influence the probability that a particular application will be adopted by an organization. Determinants of adoptability are classified into four conceptual categories – organization domain, integration, risk, and need – and their relationships to adoptability analyzed from several perspectives.

The assessment of the type and nature of environmental and organizational influences on the probability that a particular application will be adopted by an organization has long been a dominant theoretical question in diffusion research.(1) Yet, as noted in Chapter 1, as the number of empirical studies of innovation has grown, increasing concern has been expressed about the unstable, noncumulative nature of the findings. These critiques note that part of the problem is that the research lumped under the rubric of "innovation studies" encompasses an array of different theoretical concerns and different approaches (Downs & Mohr, 1976; Havelock, 1969; Warner, 1974; Yin, et al., 1976). In this chapter we employ a methodological approach which aims to overcome some of the shortcomings in the existing research and which might generate more cumulative findings.

---

*This chapter was co-authored by James Danziger, Associate Professor, School of Social Sciences, University of California, Irvine.

THE INNOVATION-DECISION DESIGN

To study adoptability, Downs and Mohr (1976: 706) propose an innovation-decision design in which the unit of analysis is "the organization with respect to a particular innovation" or "the innovation with respect to a particular organization." The number of case observations using such a design would be equal to the number of innovations times the number of organizations. Downs and Mohr (1976: 706) observe that the innovation-decision design serves to focus "attention on the shifting incentives and constraints that are relevant to the decision to innovate."

While Downs and Mohr's approach does give us a general framework, the selection and operationalization of the variables meant to explain variation in adoptability is problematic because so many different sets of independent variables are employed in innovation research. Even if one examines only the research on public agencies at the local level, the alternatives are extensive. The study by Yin, et al. (1976), which aimed to examine and codify the many empirical findings on state and local government innovation, underscores the diversity of explanatory variables. Recent research by Feller and Menzel (1976, 1975) and by Bingham (1975a) also identify arrays of variables relevant to the adoption of innovations by local government organizations. Several recent studies have also explicitly examined variables associated with the adoption of computer applications by local governments (Danziger & Dutton, 1977; Perry & Kraemer, 1978).

Thus, while we are guided by the variables identified in the other research, we replace the many specific variables with a smaller number of more abstract dimensions. Employing a small number of general concepts in the study of adoptability has several advantages. First, using a small number of abstract dimensions facilitates exploring contingent relationships among key variables in the adoption process. Several studies suggest the plausibility, for example, of interaction among variables such as motivation and resources and executive ideology and autonomy (Downs, 1976; Mohr, 1969). These types of contingent relationships become extremely difficult to isolate, however, when analyzing a large number of collinear variables. Limiting the analysis to a small number of dimensions allows contingent relationships to be more easily isolated and explored. Using a small number of general concepts also avoids problems of complex interaction created when a large number of variables are used to study innovation (Downs, 1976: 130).

CONCEPTUAL FRAMEWORK

Based on our analysis of the literature, we developed the framework of this analysis, shown in Fig. 8 (in italics). Data for the selection of variables to measure the concepts in the model, described below, were primarily derived from the URBIS survey of local government computing, with some data also drawn from Datapro 70, URISA, Datamation, and Computer World (Appendix 1).

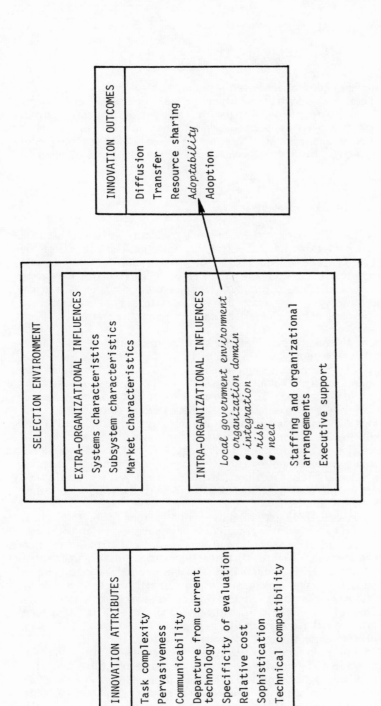

Figure 8. EXPANSION OF THE LOCAL GOVERNMENT ENVIRONMENT COMPONENT OF THE CONCEPTUAL MODEL[a]

[a]The variables in italics represent the specific portion of the analytic model examined in this chapter.

Dependent Variables

Measures of the number of innovations within a set of organizations were derived from responses identifying which of 261 functional areas were currently (1975) automated. From this list we selected ten for this analysis. The key criterion employed for selection was to maximize variations in the diffusion patterns of applications. This assured a representative sample of applications and served to maximize variations in the attributes of applications.(2)

Independent Variables

A relatively lengthy list of relevant independent variables used in innovation research is presented in Appendix 2. Based on our analysis of the literature, we first operationalized the variables and organized them in terms of the four conceptual dimensions shown in Fig. 8: relation of the innovation to organizational domain, integration, risk, and need. Variables in each group were then factor analyzed to reduce the variables to a smaller number of concepts. The four conceptual dimensions and the factors derived from them are described next.

It is important to specify the relationship of the technological innovation to an organization's domain. Domain refers to an organization's sphere of activity — that is, the technologies employed, population served, and services rendered by an organization (Thompson, 1967). Warren elaborates that domain ". . . includes the organization's access to both input and output resources, . . . it includes not only those resources needed for task performance . . . but also those needed for maintenance of the organization itself . . ." (Warren, 1972: 22). Within this broad conceptual notion, our theoretical concern is to specify the context of use for the technology, given the organizational domain. In particular, the technology might serve task performance functions and/or system maintenance functions, it might have either limited or pervasive impact on the organizational domain, and it might be used either more or less frequently.

The second conceptual dimension, integration, refers to factors which facilitate the discovery and implementation of an innovation by an organization. We expect that adoption is contingent upon awareness of the innovation and the ability to successfully internalize the innovation into organizational practice (Yin & Quick, 1977). Communication about the innovation might be facilitated by such factors as linkages into professional colleague networks and the proximity of suppliers of the technology. The capacity to successfully implement the innovation might be contingent upon the skill levels among current staff and upon the compatibility between the innovation and other technologies currently employed by the organization.

The dimension of risk incorporates those factors which influence the perception that the innovation will produce expected results.(3) Among the factors which might be considered are the financial costs of the innovation (relative to the organization's total budget and relative to other possible innovations), the availability of slack resources, and the specificity with which the innovation can be evaluated. The assumption is that organizational decision makers will undertake, directly or implicitly, a calculation of expected benefits and costs. The probability of adoption is expected to increase with decreases in the ambiguity of results and in the relative costliness of the innovation.

The need for an innovation includes both objective factors and subjective assessments of the organizational requirements to be met by the innovation. In the absence of a profitability criterion for selection of public technologies, decision makers must rely on other indicators. Need provides a substitute in that it identifies benefits that can be expected given the innovation's functional capabilities. Thus, the adoption of a computerized innovation will be more likely to the extent that it is responsive to the organization's need to perform an information processing task with greater rapidity, greater complexity, higher volume, or greater efficiency, or to the extent that managers are "optimistic" about its contributions.

Eight factors were derived from factor analyses of the variable groupings: task-maintenance orientation of the innovation, professional infrastructure, staff competence, visibility of the innovation, supplier proximity, external funding, agency dominance, and uncertainty. No factor was derived from the need variables, so two single indicators, need and perceived effectiveness of the user agency, were retained for statistical analysis. The factor loadings for the first three sets of variables are displayed in Table 20.

For the innovations in this analysis one might hypothesize various forms of the relationships between adoptability and the four dimensions and the factors derived from them. We agree with those who suspect that these relationships might be non-linear functions (Downs & Mohr, 1976); Fig. 9 presents our best estimation of these relationships. We predict that adoptability will increase positively and linearly as the relation of the innovation to organizational domain shifts from primarily task activities to maintenance activities. Adoptability should be a positive, S-curve type function of integration. Throughout the lower range of integration the probability of adoption should be quite low; at high values of integration, adoptability should be quite high. We also predict that at some point adoptability will drop precipitously as the level of risk increases. Finally, adoptability is hypothesized to be an exponential function of the need dimension.

RESEARCH METHODOLOGY

Given the ten applications and approximately 350 governmental units for which there were data, our analysis employs an N of about 3,500 cases (i.e., 10 innovations times 350 organizations). Four steps were taken to assess the relationships between the dimensions and variables identified and adoptability.

First, the individual components of the integration, risk, and need dimensions were standardized and summed so that they, as well as the conceptual dimensions, could be treated as explanatory variables. Graphic representations of relationships between adoptability and the explanatory variables were developed, using cross tabulations between the dichotomized dependent variable and each of the independent variables.

Table 20. FACTOR LOADINGS AND DEFINITIONS FOR THE DOMAIN, INTEGRATION, AND RISK VARIABLES

A. DOMAIN VARIABLES

	Task-Maintenance Orientation of the Innovation — Characterizes the application along a continuum ranging from intensive use in agency task-related activities to occasional use in organization-wide maintenance activities.
Frequency of generation	-.54
Frequency of use	-.86
Transitivity	.65
Pervasiveness	.75

B. INTEGRATION VARIABLES

	Professional Infrastructure — Extent of interpersonal communication channels with external reference groups	Staff Competence — Amount of technical competence of the organization's data processing staff.	Supplier Proximity — The proximity of computer mainframe and service suppliers.
Professional communication	.00	.00	.00
Relative earliness of an application's first adoption		.00	.00
URISA membership	.93	-.06	.01
URISA conference attendance	.98	-.03	.03
Computer manufacturer mainframe sales offices	-.04	.09	.63
Computer service supplier sales office	.07	.01	.68
Staff experience	-.00	.74	.18
Staff skill level	-.07	.72	-.04

C. RISK VARIABLES

	External Funding — Extent of financial resources for computing from external sources.	Agency Dominance — Relative status of the potential adopting agency as indicated by its share of local government resources.	Uncertainty — Degree of certainty that the results desired from adopting an application will be obtained.
Specificity of evaluation	.00	-.01	.37
Cost relative to other agency applications	.00	-.05	-.38
Agency expenditures	.01	.47	.06
Agency expenditure as a percentage of total government unit expenditure	.02	.47	-.01
External funding of EDP	.67	.01	.00
External funding of EDP as a percentage of total EDP budget	.68	.03	.00

Statistical techniques were then used to assess the strength and significance of associations between adoptability and the variables. Zero-order correlation and multiple regression analysis were employed. Finally, interactive effects among the four conceptual dimensions were evaluated by using controls to stratify the values on each dimension.

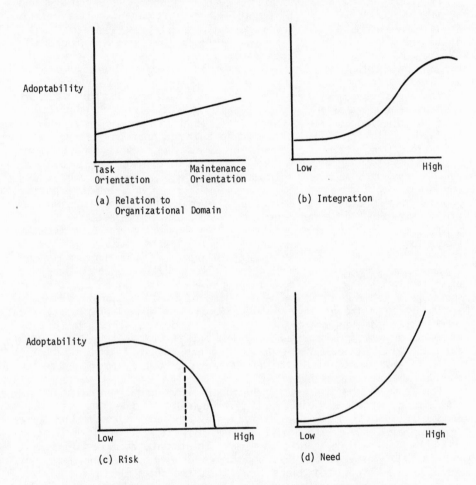

Figure 9.   HYPOTHESIZED RELATIONSHIPS BETWEEN THE FOUR CONCEPTUAL DIMENSIONS AND ADOPTABILITY

RESEARCH FINDINGS

The Shape of the Relationships Between the Conceptual Dimensions and Adoptability

The shape of the relationships between the conceptual dimensions and actual configurations of the adoptability-conceptual dimension relationships are displayed in Fig. 10. The area under each curve represents the probability of adoption. It is clear that only the curve for the integration dimension closely corresponds to our expectations. Except at the lowest and highest levels of integration, adoptability increases as a relatively linear function of greater integration.

The operational relationship between an innovation's adoptability and its relation to organizational domain in Fig. 10 is particularly intriguing. Rather than the expected linear relationship, the actual configuration is roughly an inverted-U. This curvilinear relationship suggests that innovations which relate to either purely task aspects or purely maintenance aspects of an organization's domain are less likely to be adopted than those innovations which serve both task and maintenance functions. The task end of this dimension, it should be recalled, involves applications which impact primarily upon the particular agency, which do not disturb organizational arrangements, and which respond to frequently recurring information processing needs of the unit. From a bureaucratic self-interest perspective, this is the type of innovation that would, ceteris paribus, be most attractive to the agency. However, the scarcity of EDP resources in most local governments and the value attributed by resource allocators to "organization-wide" efficiencies often result in a bias toward developing applications that benefit a wider spectrum of government actors. Given these intra-organizational realities, it is plausible that the most generalized support and highest priorities would tend to gravitate to those applications which appear to serve a mixture of maintenance- and task-oriented functions. This is, in fact, what Fig. 10 (a) suggests. While some highly task-oriented applications have a reasonable probability of adoption, it is the middle ranges of this dimension where the probability of adoption is highest.

The form of the risk relationship bears only partial similarity to the relationship hypothesized in Fig. 9. Through the middle range of risk, adoptability does decrease with increasing risk, although not as precipitously as anticipated.   At high levels of risk, however, adoptability remains relatively constant with increasing risk. These data are consistent with Feller's (1977) suggestion that innovators in public agencies are not particularly averse to risk, since institutional characteristics in the governmental context minimize the change that innovation "failures" will be discovered and/or that those responsible will be identified and sanctioned. However, at lower levels of risk, adoptability actually decreases with decreasing risk.

The Shape of the Relationships Between
the Component Factors and Adoptability

Graphic representations of the component factors of the integration, risk, and need dimensions are presented in Fig. 11.

With regard to the integration components, the most critical relationship is the substantial increase in innovation adoptability with higher levels of visibility. This linkage suggests that an innovation has a higher probability of adoption if it has enjoyed greater attention in professional media and if it was introduced relatively early. Clearly, these circumstances should make the innovation more accessible and comprehensible to potential adopters.

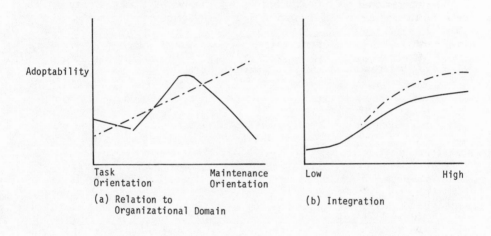

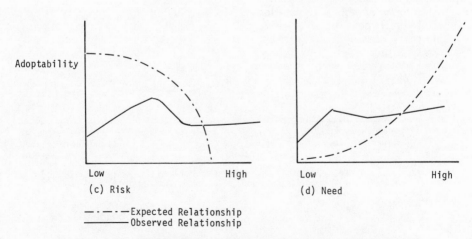

—·—·—Expected Relationship
————— Observed Relationship

Figure 10.   OPERATIONAL RELATIONSHIPS BETWEEN THE FOUR CONCEPTUAL DIMENSIONS AND ADOPTABILITY

There is a clear positive relationship between adoptability and the component of risk termed external funding. The presence of slack resources provided by an outside funding agency facilitates the adoption of the innovative device, a result consistent with many other studies of innovation and with the studies of computer innovation. Although agency dominance has

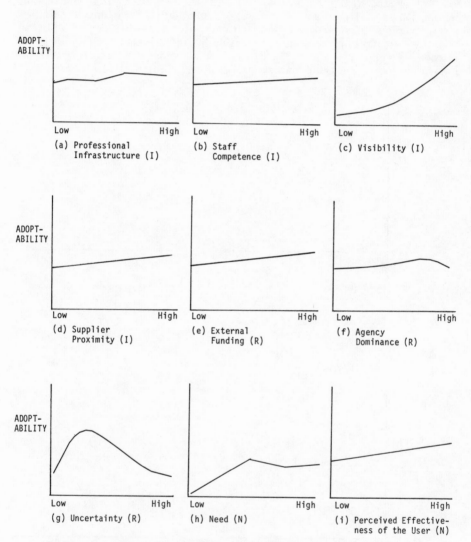

Figure 11. OPERATIONAL RELATIONSHIPS BETWEEN ADOPTABILITY AND THE INDIVIDUAL COMPONENTS OF INTEGRATION (I), RISK (R), AND NEED (N)

no clear relationship to adoptability, the risk component we have termed uncertainty has a most interesting configuration. From mid-low to high levels, the uncertainty variable's relationship to adoptability is fully consistent with the expectation that the probability of adoption decreases as uncertainty about the cost-benefit ratio and likely success of the innovation increases. However, adoptability also drops sharply at the lowest levels of uncertainty. That is, where the cost of this automated application (relative to the cost of others) is low and where quite specific evaluation of the application is possible, the probability of adoption is reduced.

There is no obvious explanation for this unexpected finding regarding adoptability and low uncertainty. Perhaps there is a type of trivializing-the-innovation rationale among adopters – that if the magnitude of costs and benefits is small, then the innovation is not worth the effort. A more plausible explanation is that the very fact that specific evaluation of the innovation can be undertaken is viewed by potential adopters as a negative factor. If the potential adopter believes that a clear assessment of shortcomings in production efficiency could be undertaken, the innovation might seem less desirable since a "failure" would be difficult to obfuscate (Feller, 1977).

Examination of the need components reveals several additional relationships. The perceived effectiveness of the user represents a subjective appraisal by the chief executive of a specific agency's production efficiency in the use of automated applications. The relationship in Fig. 10(i) indicates that further adoptions are most likely in those agencies that are judged to have been most effective in applying the technology in the past. The objective measure of need for each specific automated application reveals that, across the entire set of innovations, increased need is related to increased adoptability only at the lower levels of need.

Statistical Assessment of the Relationships

All of the zero-order correlations between adoption and each of the independent variables in Fig. 11 were statistically significant (at the .001 level) except professional infrastructure and agency dominance. However, the magnitude of most of the linear correlations was quite low, and significance was often due to large sample size. There were two notable associations – adoptability was substantially associated with visibility ($r = +.38$) and somewhat associated with uncertainty ($r = .13$).

The graphic analyses in Fig. 11 also suggested that some of the relationships with adoptability of innovations might be non-linear. Consequently, certain transformations were attempted for the variables of domain, visibility, uncertainty, and need.(4) An exponential transformation did not markedly improve the relationship of visibility and adoptability and a transformation of the need variable improved its correlation with adoptability slightly (from +.06 to +.09). A transformation of the domain variable altered its correlation with adoptability from .03 to -.07. There was also a quite substantial improvement in the correlation between adoptability and a transformation of the uncertainty variable. This association increased from -.13 for the original values to -.32 for a transformation accounting for the curve at the low uncertainty level.

To evaluate the independent contributions of the individual component variables of the integration, risk, and need dimensions, multiple regression techniques were used. Table 21 reports the results of multiple regression analyses for the component variables of each dimension, taking adoption as the dependent variable. Among the dimensions, it is evident that integration is the most powerful explanatory dimension, since it explains about 15 percent of the variance in adoptability (as measured by the R^2 statistic). Among the component factors of integration, visibility of the innovation is clearly the most significant one. Consistent with earlier inferences, there is a considerable increase in the probability of adoption for an innovation which has been the subject of more extensive professional communication and which has had an earlier introduction. The risk dimension explains 10 percent of the variation in adoptability and is primarily a function of the uncertainty factor, which has a quite significant association with adoptability. It is also clear that the components of the need dimension have minimal explanatory power regarding adoptability.

The final column in Table 21 reports the multiple regression solution for the variation in innovation adoption, utilizing all the significant component variables in the analysis. This equation reveals that there are substantial, independent contributions to adoptability by the variables identified earlier as being important. The probability of innovation adoption tends to increase where: 1) the innovation is more visible; 2) there is less uncertainty regarding its evaluation and cost; 3) the innovation is more maintenance-oriented than task-oriented; 4) there is greater objective need (in a production efficiency sense) for the innovation; and 5) suppliers of computer services are more proximate to the adopting government. The optimal linear combination of these variables, along with several others (that are not statistically significant), explains 25 percent of the variance in adoption.

Assessing Interactions Among the Four Dimensions

If there are contingent relationships among the explanatory variables, it is likely that a linear statistical model such as that used above underestimates the variance explained by these four dimensions. Given this possibility, it is useful to explore the conditional relationships among the four conceptual dimensions.

To test for interactions among the four dimensions in their associations with the adoptability of innovations, each dimension was stratified into high and low categories. The criterion for inclusion was to retain for the analysis only those values more than one-half standard deviation above or below the mean. That is, the data in each part of Table 22 are based on only those cases which met this criterion on the relevant stratifying variable. The table reports the fraction of explained variance (the R^2) in adoptability accounted for by each of the other three dimensions, stratifying on the fourth.

When the organizational domain variable is used to stratify the cases, there are several striking results. Table 22 reveals that the relationship between adoptability and the need dimension is not contingent upon the domain dimension, but the effect of organizational domain on the explanatory power of the other two dimensions is substantial. The integration dimension is able to explain about 50 percent more variance when the task-maintenance

Table 21. MULTIPLE LINEAR REGRESSIONS FOR THE COMPONENTS OF EACH CONCEPTUAL DIMENSION AND ADOPTION

Variable	Domain Variable	Integration Variables	Risk Variables	Need Variables	All Significant Factors
Task-maintenance orientation of the innovation (transformed)	-.07***				.19***
Professional Infrastructure		.00			.03
Staff Competence		.07***			.32***
Visibility		.37***			.05**
Supplier Proximity		.07***			.02
External Funding			.04*		
Agency Dominance			.01		
Uncertainty (transformed)			-.31***	.08***	-.33***
Need (transformed)				.03	
Perceived Effectiveness of the User Agency					
Constant	.35	.34	.52	-.61	-.26
R^2	.07	.15	.10	.01	.25
F	18.42***	116.24***	83.22***	8.49***	101.41***

*p < .05
**p < .025
***p < .01

Table 22. R^2's FOR THREE OF THE DIMENSIONS WHEN STRATIFIED BY
SCORES OF THE FOURTH DIMENSION

	Relation to Organizational Domain			Integration	
	Low	High		Low	High
Integration	.19	.12	Relation to organizational domain	.00	.00
Risk	.02	.44	Risk	.05	.15
Need	.04	.00	Need	.02	.01

	Risk			Need	
	Low	High		Low	High
Relation to organizational domain	.15	.01	Relation to organizational domain	.00	.01
Integration	.17	.14	Integration	.15	.08
Risk	.01	.01	Risk	.01	.06

orientation values are low than when they are high. A dramatic difference also occurs with the risk dimension, where the R^2 for adoptability and risk is only +.02 for low values of the domain dimension but is +.44 for high values.

These results suggest that when an application relates to task accomplishment aspects of an organization's domain (that is, when the innovation primarily serves a recurrent task activity within a single agency), factors relating to the visibility and successful implementation of the innovation are particularly important. But the level of risk and, we infer, the magnitude of benefits relative to costs and the probability of failure, have no consistent linear effect on decisions regarding such task-oriented applications. These findings are consistent with Feller's contention that consideration of the cost/benefit shortcomings of an innovation is not necessarily a major constraint when the innovation is internal to the agency. Since the innovation tends to impact only the specific agency (in our analysis, a task-oriented application), the agency is able to cover the failure of an innovation. Feller argues that for such an innovation, failure is most likely to be defined in terms of failure to implement successfully rather than shortcomings in eventual benefits. Thus the motivation to adopt the task-oriented innovation relates more to implementation issues (integration) than to impact considerations (risk).

When one examines the more maintenance-oriented innovations, as opposed to the task-oriented ones, risk becomes the critical dimension. While the implementation considerations inferred from the integration dimension have some influence, the concern with magnitude of costs relative to benefits and with uncertainty of impacts is central. One explanation of the centrality of risk to maintenance-oriented applications pivots upon the composition of "interested and attentive parties." When the application is maintenance-oriented, it will have direct or indirect impacts on a wider spectrum of actors both within and external to the agency primarily responsible for its utilization. For example, an automated current balance report system implemented by the finance department will generate financial information which is distributed to all operating agencies. Thus, there are multiple actors who are motivated to attend to the impacts of the innovation as it is routinized and who are capable of evaluating the substance and quality of its impacts. Given the existence of multiple actors who can assess impacts, the adopting agency is likely to be considerably more concerned that the inadequate performance of an innovation could be discovered and communicated. In this case, those who are most accountable for the innovation's impacts (and who are typically the pivotal advocates for adoption) will tend to be much more responsible to consideration of risk.

When cases are stratified on the basis of high and low scores on the integration dimension, other types of interactions are evident. The relationship of adoptability and the level of integration does not seem to be contingent upon either the organizational domain or the need dimensions. Risk does account for a substantially greater proportion of the variance in adoptability when integration is high rather than low. Higher integration implies that there is more visibility, comprehension, and staff competency regarding the implementation and use of the innovation. In such cases, it should be possible to make a more accurate assessment of the implications of risk and also to react more "rationally," or at least more sensibly, to those implications. When integration is low, on the other hand, there is limited understanding and technical insight about the innovation, and adoption decisions are likely to be more strongly influenced by criteria or attitudes that ignore or misperceive the factors or risk. Thus, high integration is likely to complement the importance of risk, but low integration might limit its salience to adoption decisions.

The risk dimension has limited interactive effects with two of the three conceptual dimensions in their relationship with adoptability. The need dimension is not systematically associated with adoptability at either the high or the low levels of risk. And the integration dimension seems to be an important determinant of adoptability regardless of whether risk is high or low. However, stratifying the cases by risk underlines the interaction effects between risk and the relation to organizational domain. Under conditions of high risk, the domain orientation of the automated application accounts for very little variance in adoptability. That is, neither task- nor maintenance-oriented innovations are more consistently deterred when risk and uncertainty about impacts are high. But when risk is low, relation to domain accounts for 15 percent of the variance. Specifically, the probability of adoption of the more maintenance-oriented innovations increases if they are low risk. This is further evidence that as the impacts of an innovation are more pervasive and there are more interested and attentive parties, adopters are most favorably disposed toward those innovations characterized by a minimum of risk to the adopting unit.

When the cases are stratified by need there is no alteration in the relationship between adoptability and organizational domain, but the integration and risk variables are affected by the level of need. The integration dimension explains twice the variance in adoptability when need is low as when need is high. It seems that the innovation's visibility, staff competence, and supplier proximity are likely to create some pressures/inducements for adoption even when there is little apparent need (as measured by a specific, production efficiency indicator). In contrast, at high levels of need the decision to adopt is less contingent upon the level of integration in the organization. There is also slight evidence that when need is greater, there is more willingness to take larger risks in the attempt to realize the potential benefits of the innovation. High need moderates the constraint of greater risk, while the level of integration becomes a more important factor when need is low. Need has no systematic influence on the adoptability-organizational domain linkage. As in the early analyses, Table 22 provides little evidence that innovation decisions are particularly contingent upon need.

DISCUSSION

At a substantive level, many findings in this analysis are intriguing. Four broad conceptual dimensions which might explain variations in adoptability of innovations were identified and operationalized. The relevant explanatory variables were classified in terms of these four dimensions and then were reduced into a smaller set of factors characteristic of each dimension. Of these eight individual factors and two indicators of need, seven had statistical associations with adoptability that were significant. When all factors were regressed in a single analysis, four were particularly important. Higher probability of adoption for an innovative computer application associated with: 1) greater visibility of the innovation; 2) less uncertainty about the cost and evaluation of the innovation; 3) greater staff competence to implement the innovation; and 4) a higher level of objective need for the innovation.

The combination of graphic and statistical analyses suggested interesting differences among the four conceptual dimensions. Of the four, the integration dimension has the highest independent explanatory power for variation in adoptability of the innovations. Integration is also the most obviously linear of the four dimensions, and adoptability increases as a function of greater organizational integration. Among the components of integration, it is clear that the visibility of the innovation increases the attention afforded the innovation and enhances the adopters' sense that they understand its implications for local government operations. In addition, higher staff competence might increase both comprehension and also the level of conviction that the innovation can be successfully developed and implemented.

The risk dimension also displays considerable explanatory power for variation in adoptability among the innovations. This dimension's effect corresponds broadly to the intuitive notion that as risk is greater – that is, as there is more uncertainty about an innovation's costs and benefits and more dependence on internal development funding – the probability of adoption tends to diminish. However, the data reflect that at the lower levels of risk there is also a reduction in adoptability. While we offered several plausible explanations for this finding, primarily relating to the peculiar limitations upon the risk constraint in public organizations, these relationships merit further research.

It is also evident that adoptability varies substantially with respect to the organizational domain dimension. The graphic representation suggests that an innovation is most adoptable when it satisfies a mixture of task and maintenance functions. Such an application is desirable to the individual unit most directly served, since both advocacy of and responsibility for the innovation can be spread, yet the unit remains the primary beneficiary. This kind of adoption also is favored by other units which enjoy indirect benefits, and by central decision makers who might see the adoption as serving broader organizational interests. It is the more pervasive, maintenance-oriented applications that are most powerfully influenced by the level of risk, since multiple actors are in a position to evaluate the effectiveness of the innovation and of the adopting agency's utilization of it. While a more risky maintenance-oriented application is likely to find few promoters, a risky task-oriented innovation might be advocated by an agency which reckons that no outsiders will be capable of evaluating the agency's success or failure. Indeed, among task-oriented applications, the least adoptable ones are those which are subject to the most specific and unambiguous impact evaluation.

The fourth dimension, need, has the weakest associations with adoptability. Our specific measures of objective need for the applications (relative to other local governments' need for the same application) might indicate the production efficiency (or selection environment) for the innovation. The multiple regression equation reveals that greater need has a small but significant coefficient with respect to higher probability of adoption. But the broader inference from the data is that the need dimension is much less critical to variance in adoptability than are the domain, integration, and risk dimensions.

From a public policy perspective, it seems that the adoptability of this class of innovations is responsive to some variables which can be manipulated by interventions. In particular, adoptability can be enhanced if high risk can be moderated, especially for high-need innovations. This might be accomplished by the provision of considerable external funding support or by lowering the relative cost of the application in some other manner (such as the presence of an effective program for software transfer). Adoptability also seems to be affected by the visibility of the innovation. Thus, an innovation is more likely to be adopted when communication about it is facilitated within professional peer networks or when an efficient information "clearinghouse" for automated systems is instituted. These findings also suggest that the dynamics among key determinants of adoptability differ between task- and maintenance-oriented applications. Hence, attempts to manipulate the integration dimension for task-oriented applications and the risk dimension for maintenance-oriented applications increase the probability of stimulating adoption decisions.

CONCLUSION

While, for the most part, our use of organization domain, integration, risk, and need as explanatory adoption dimensions did not support the explicit relationships we had anticipated, our results did show that they had signficant influences on adoptability. Five components of these dimensions made significant contributions to the explanation of variation in application adoption: task-maintenance orientation of the innovation, visibility, supplier proximity, uncertainty, and need.

Even more significant results were obtained from our analysis of interactions among the four conceptual dimensions. These suggested that: staff competence, the innovation's visibility, and supplier availability are important factors, particularly when the application relates to task accomplishment; that risk becomes an important determinant of adoptability when an application is maintenance oriented; and that the organization's integration and the uses to which the application is put become important determining factors when adoption decisions involve minimal risks.

5 Staffing and Organizational Influences

Although researchers have increasingly acknowledged that chief executives exert important influences on innovation decisions, many of the determinants of that role are still unclear. This chapter employs several implicit models in the literature to develop an explicit model of the influences of executive participation and other organizational processes on innovation adoption. Path analysis is then used to test the plausibility of the model.

Recent analyses of technological innovations in local government have shown some consensus on the importance of "overhead" influences, such as chief executive support, in adoption processes. Yet, many of the determinants of these influences and the precise impacts that they exert on innovation decisions are still unclear. Since local government chief executives are indeed important overhead influences, an understanding of the processes by which executive support influences innovation outcomes is an important component in our understanding of those outcomes. Our approach here is.to develop an explicit model of the executive's influence in innovation adoption based on implicit models in the literature.

MODELS OF ORGANIZATIONAL INNOVATION

Although the literature abounds with models of organizational innovation, two general models are readily identifiable. We call these prototypes the organizational structure and organizational process models. While these models are not, in most instances, mutually exclusive, they are distinguishable foci of research. The organizational structure model focuses on the association between attributes of organization structure (e.g., size and

91

differentiation) and innovation as an organizational outcome (Hage & Aiken, 1967; Moch, 1976). The rationale for the structural models of organizational innovation is that organizational structure sets the parameters for activities which influence decisions to adopt or not to adopt a new technology. Organizational structure may itself be contingent upon environmental factors so the structural theorists frequently incorporate "open" systems features into their models.

The contrasting organizational process model focuses on innovative behavior in organizations and the conditions which surround it. Individual and group processes are emphasized rather than macro-structural factors. Critical variables from the perspective of the process theorists are slack resources, structural looseness, group processes, professionalism, and freedom from unusual external pressures (Thompson, 1965). This model tends to view innovation more as a function of internal organization dynamics than as a result ultimately of environmental contingencies.

Within this theoretical context, we reviewed studies on government innovation that explicitly considered the chief executive's role in the innovation process. The role of the chief executive in local government innovation has been approached primarily from the organizational process perspective. A summary of the concepts and propositions encountered in the literature is provided in Table 23.

CONCEPTUAL FRAMEWORK

The review of the literature serves two purposes in the present analysis. First, it is useful for defining or suggesting concepts relevant to chief executive influence in innovation. The discussion in this chapter focuses on variables suggested in the literature and the more general concepts they represent. Second, statements from the literature assist in defining the causal ordering among variables in a model of chief executive influence on innovation adoption.

Figure 12 shows the variables (in italics) and relationships drawn from the concepts presented in Table 23. Data used to measure these variables are largely drawn from the URBIS survey described in Appendix 1.

Dependent Variables

The conceptualization of innovation outcomes in the studies in Table 23 implies a consistent definition of innovation as "the successful introduction into an applied situation of means or ends that are new to that situation" (Mohr, 1969: 112). Recent research suggests that innovation is a multidimensional concept which includes adoption, implementation, and use (Rogers & Eveland, 1976). As conceptualized in the studies in Table 23, top management's role in the innovation process is confined primarily to adoption. However, the references of these studies to two different levels of impact — the organization and organizational subunits — indicates executive support may influence both the magnitude (frequency) and scope (pervasiveness) of innovation. Innovation magnitude represents the number of adoptions within

TABLE 23. SUMMARY OF PROPOSITIONS RELATING EXECUTIVE SUPPORT TO INNOVATION IN GOVERNMENT ORGANIZATIONS

	PROPOSITIONS			
Author(s)	Organizational Climate	Resources	Decision-making Process	Innovation Outcomes
Feller & Menzel (1975)	I Executive branch pressures on agencies to restrain budgets and improve productivity		Agency search for labor-saving techniques	
	II Executive support of specific techniques			Agency innovation
Mohr (1969)	III Executive motivation to innovate			Innovation adoption/ progressive programming
Radnor, Rubenstein & Tansik (1970)	IV Top-management support of the project and the project's entire context		Client willingness to support implementation	
	V Top-management support of the project and of the project's entire context	Availability of money and personnel for implementation		
	VI Top-management system of variables — Top-management support of the project and of the project's entire context			
	VII Relevant past outcomes — Top-management support of the project and of the project's entire context			
Yin, et al. (1976)	VIII Chief executive support			Innovation incorporation

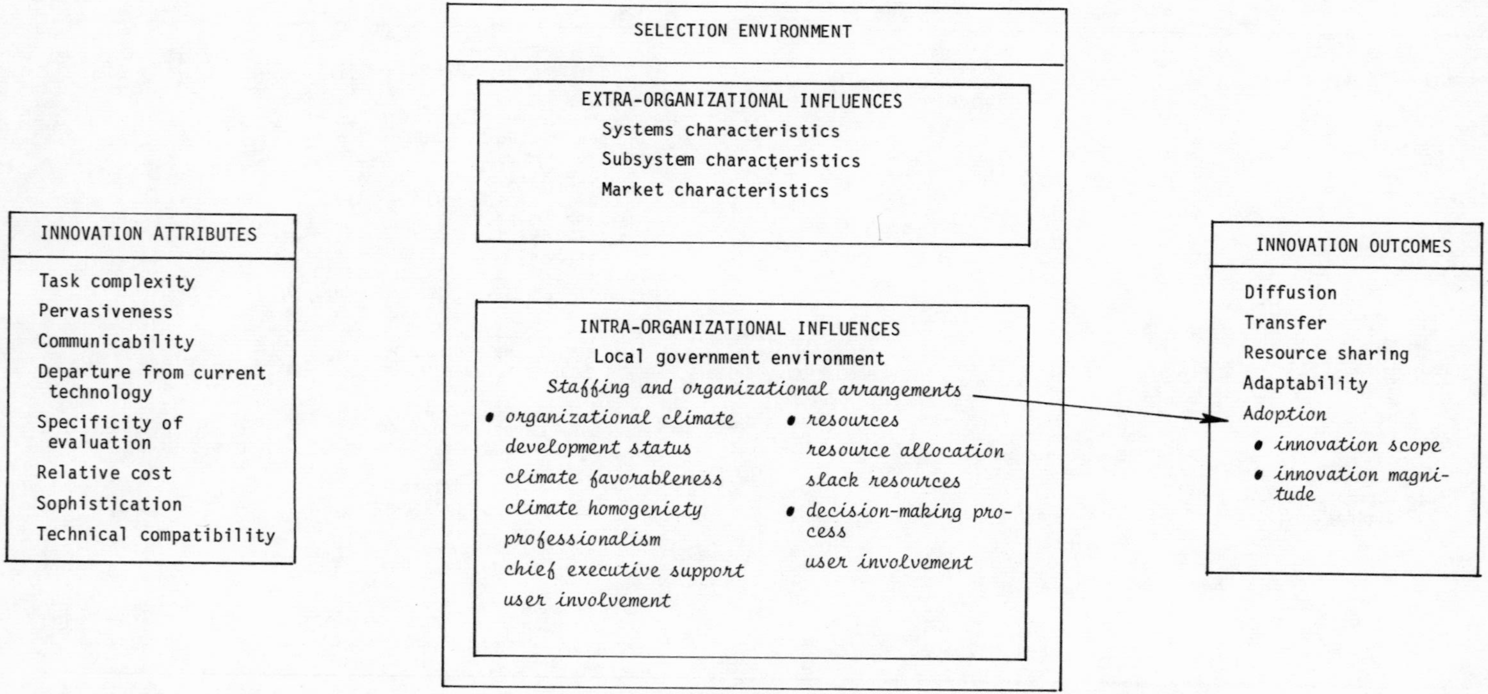

INNOVATION ATTRIBUTES

Task complexity
Pervasiveness
Communicability
Departure from current
technology
Specificity of
evaluation
Relative cost
Sophistication
Technical compatibility

SELECTION ENVIRONMENT

EXTRA-ORGANIZATIONAL INFLUENCES

Systems characteristics
Subsystem characteristics
Market characteristics

INTRA-ORGANIZATIONAL INFLUENCES

Local government environment

Staffing and organizational arrangements
- *organizational climate*
- *resources*
  development status   resource allocation
  climate favorableness   slack resources
  climate homogeniety   • *decision-making pro-*
  professionalism   *cess*
  chief executive support   user involvement
  user involvement

INNOVATION OUTCOMES

Diffusion
Transfer
Resource sharing
Adaptability
Adoption
- *innovation scope*
- *innovation magni-*
  tude

Figure 12. EXPANSION OF THE STAFFING AND ORGANIZATIONAL ARRANGEMENTS COMPONENTS OF THE ANALYTIC MODEL[a]

[a]The variables in italics represent the specific portion of the
analytic model examined in this chapter.

the organization; innovation scope refers to the distribution of innovation across organizational subunits.

Independent Variables

Organizational climate generally denotes the internal environment of an organization. Rogers and Agarwala-Rogers (1976: 75) note that "an organization's climate exerts a strong influence on its members' behavior." However, their brief mention of the concept does not convey the multiplicity of meanings assigned to the term. Organizational climate is used predominantly as an organizing concept for a cluster of internal organizational variables which are considered generally to affect behavior by influencing "the valences attached to certain outcomes, the instrumentalities for these outcomes, and expectations for various strategies to achieve these outcomes" (James & Jones, 1974: 1096-97).

The summary of propositions in Table 23 suggests three dimensions of organizational climate relevant to the innovation adoption process. Propositions I and III represent general executive pressures or norms that stimulate technological innovation. The specific variables emphasized in the literature – restraints on budgets, emphasis on productivity, and motivation to innovate – suggest the more general notion of professionalism. Professional norms may contribute to innovation by encouraging organizational members to maintain familiarity with new techniques and methods in their fields, by enhancing efficient use of resources so that slack may be created for innovative activity, and by facilitating objective assessments of problems or performance gaps.

Propositions II, IV, V and VIII deal directly with the influence of executive support for a specific technology. The varying units used in these propositions – "executive branch," "top-management," "chief executive" – suggest the importance of several sources of executive support. The chief executive's support may be crucial because of his control of discretionary resources and the legitimacy the chief executive's support lends to any organizational activity. Simultaneously, the favorableness of the climate created by legislative and department head support of a particular technology will probably also influence member behavior.

In their discussion of management science implementation, Radnor, Rubenstein and Tansik (1970) introduce two concepts they believe are associated with executive support: the top-management system of variables and relevant past outcomes. Although these concepts are not fully defined in their study, it might be inferred from their use that the top-management system of variables refers to the homogeneity of top management support and relevant past outcomes refers to the development status of the technology within the organization. Homogeneity of support should probably influence the willingness of lower level organizational members to initiate and follow through on innovative activities as well as reduce the likelihood of deadlock in decision making among organizational leaders. The developmental status of the technology will influence the availability of the "critical mass" of resources necessary for innovation and the "routinization" of innovation processes.

Proposition V (Table 23) links top management support to the availability of resources required for innovation. The availability of resources may refer to either of two uses of the resource concept which are prominent in the innovation literature. First, there is the notion of resource allocation for innovative activity, what Rogers and Agarwala-Rogers (1976: 161) term "deliberately created" resources "that are not committed to other purposes." This might be considered the distributive connotation of the term.(1) A second notion, slack resources, refers to resources in a redistributive sense. Slack resources represent underutilized or unproductive resources already committed to activities within the organization (Cyert & March, 1963; Yin, et al., 1976). Slack resources frequently refers both to the ability of the organization to create new resources and to its ability to reallocate existing resources.(2)

Propositions I and IV (Table 23) suggest that executive pressures and top-management support stimulate two types of behavior by lower-level organizational participants — search for labor-saving techniques and willingness to support innovation implementation. These two concepts can be conceived more generally as user involvement or participation in the innovation process. Yin, et al. (1976: 150) while not directly linking chief executive support to user involvement, note that "the most important implementation factor was the presence of client participation, though some evidence was found that practitioner training was also important." Hage and Aiken (1967) similarly found a strong positive relationship between participation in agency-wide decisions and program change in 16 social welfare organizations.

RESEARCH METHODOLOGY

By specifying the relationships among the variables that are not causally ordered (e.g., resource allocation and slack resources), path analysis can be used to test the plausibility of the model derived from the propositions in Table 23. If each variable is assumed to be a linear combination of the variables that precede it in Fig. 12, only the relationships among the organizational climate variables and among the resource variables require further specification. The relationships among the five exogenous variables are treated as bidirectional correlations. Slack resources is assumed to be causally dependent upon the level of resource allocation.

In order to measure the four classes of variables in this study, relevant variables were identified and operationalized as described in Appendix 2.(3)

RESEARCH FINDINGS

The results of the path analysis for each innovation outcome are presented in Figs. 13 and 14. Since these results are important for evaluating a number of points that have already been considered, this discussion is divided into two parts: 1) the implications of the results for the propositions reviewed in Table 23, and 2) the relationship of these results to the findings of other studies on technological innovation in public organizations.

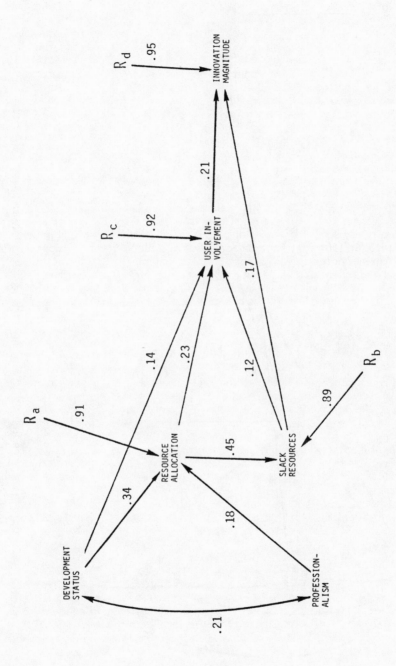

Figure 13. PATH MODEL FOR INNOVATION MAGNITUDE SHOWING SIGNIFICANT PATHS AMONG THE STUDY VARIABLES.

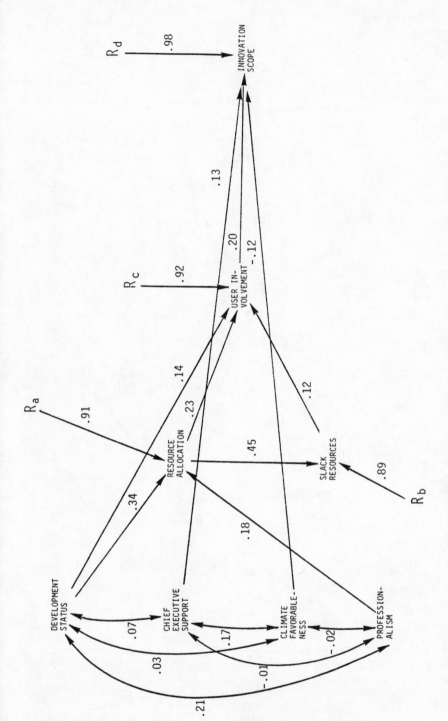

Figure 14. PATH MODEL FOR INNOVATION SCOPE SHOWING SIGNIFICANT PATHS AMONG THE STUDY VARIABLES.

Implications for Propositions on Executive Support

The two path models provide only moderate support for the set of propositions regarding executive support reviewed in Table 23. (The next chapter investigates in more detail why executive support may not be more influential.) Because climate homogeneity was not significantly related either to the intervening variables or the outcome variables, it was deleted from each path model. Similarly chief executive support and climate favorableness were deleted from the path model for innovation magnitude since they were not significantly related to any of the endogenous variables. The direct paths for chief executive support and climate favorableness, however, were significant in the innovation scope model. Because the direct paths suggested by propositions IV and V are not significant and the bidirectional correlations among the top-management variables and development status and professionalism are extremely weak, the relationships posited by Radnor, Rubenstein, and Tansik (1970) between top-management support and both resource availability and user supportiveness are not supported by these results.

Perhaps the most interesting result vis-a-vis the literature on the executive's influence in local government innovation is the contrasting signs for the paths between innovation scope and the two independent variables, chief executive support, and climate favorableness. The positive path for chief executive support is direct confirmation of proposition II in Table 23. More importantly, the differences in the results for the innovation magnitude and scope models suggest that the chief executive's support is influential, not in the frequency of computer application adoptions within the organization, but in their distribution among organizational subunits. On the other hand, the negative sign between climate favorableness and innovation scope suggests that increasing levels of elected official and department head support of data processing actually constrain the widespread adoption of computer applications.

From his analysis of the organizational politics surrounding a large-scale computer innovation in a British firm, Pettigrew (1973: 169) provides one possible rationale for explaining the negative path between climate favorableness and innovation scope:

> Political behavior is defined as behavior by individuals, or, in collective terms, by subunits, within an organization that makes a claim against the resource-sharing system of the organization. Those resources may be salaries, capital expenditure, new equipment, or control over people, information, or new areas of a business. New resources may be created and appear to fall within the jurisdiction of a department or individual who has not previously been a claimant in a particular area. Those who see their interests threatened by the change may invoke resistance in the joint decision process.

The negative relationship between climate favorableness and innovation scope may reflect the tendency for data processing innovations to reinforce and strengthen existing patterns of resource allocation. Elected officials are likely to allocate resources for data processing just as they allocate resources for other goods and services — differentially to organizational subunits in accordance with their perceptions of political advantage or need. Widespread department head support for data processing also guarantees that previously successful bureaucratic entrepreneurs may have a greater likelihood of claiming new resources. This explanation of the relationship between climate favorableness and innovation scope is consistent with the framework of bureaucratic politics and technological change that Lambright and Flynn (1976: i) observed in Syracuse and Rochester, New York:

> Adoption involves an allocation of resources to purchase new technology. In most functions, adoption is made, or legitimated, by elected officials. Bureaucratic strategies to obtain local adoption decisions owe much of their success or failure to the marketing talents of administrative leaders. To market their technologies, such leaders may utilize outside funding as bait, engage in "successful" demonstrations, use the media, and ally themselves with community interest groups. Bureaucratic entrepreneurs seek to build a system of pressures around elected officials to obtain the decisions they want.

Relationship of the Results to Those From Other Studies on Local Government Innovation

Since the model of executive influence which we tested was confined to internal organizational variables, it provides an opportunity for assessing recently made distinctions between two processes of innovation in local government organizations — political and bureaucratic (Bingham, 1975a; Yin, et al., 1976). Our finding regarding the relationship between climate favorableness and innovation scope suggests that, if two processes do exist, they cannot be strictly dichotomized. Bureaucratic innovation processes encompass political behavior. The residuals in the models we tested, however, are consistently about .90. It is possible that a good deal of the unexplained variance in the innovation outcomes may be attributable to differences in the policy systems in which local governments are imbedded.

Another recent study of local government innovation by Feller and Menzel concludes that "municipal responsiveness to new technologies is organized along functional lines, and that functional areas differ in the manner in which problems are defined, information disseminated, and resources distributed" (Feller & Menzel, 1975: 287). This study contributes a number of additional perspectives to their conclusion. Although agencies may differ in their responsiveness to innovation, functional units do respond to executive pressures and influence. Furthermore, one reason agencies may differ in their responsiveness to innovation is the political nature of internal resource allocatoin in local governments. Differential levels of innovation among agencies may be internally perpetuated by the hierarchy of subunits in the local government resource allocation system. Any external efforts to influence levels of subunit innovation within local governments will therefore have to come to grips with this process.

DISCUSSION

With regard to the general innovation literature, the results of the analysis are important in several respects. First, the path models for innovation magnitude and scope reaffirm the importance of slack resources as a variable in the innovation process. Second, while our treatment of the decision-making process was limited to a single variable, user involvement, it indicates that particular types of organizational structures influence the magnitude and scope of innovation adoption within an organization. The normative implication of this finding is that organizations could clearly enhance their capacity to innovate through the conscious design of their internal operations. Finally, the results of this analysis implicitly echo Rogers' criticism of the "psychological bias" of research on innovation in organizations. "Only recently has the main focus in diffusion research on the individual as the unit of analysis shifted to the dyad, clique, network, organization, or system of individuals; hence the relationships between individuals, rather than on the individuals themselves" (Rogers, 1975: 17). Given the competing claims for scarce resources in local government organizations, for example, we found the general level of professionalism of the organization and the status of its technological development to be much more important in the allocation of resources to technological innovation than the supportiveness of the chief executive or the receptivity of elected officials and department heads. We also found that the impact of the motivational orientation of an actor or set of actors on innovation outcomes is contingent upon an actor's organizational position. Thus, the results suggest that it is useful to conceptually distinguish between an actor's organizational position and an actor's motivational orientation when conducting research on organizational innovation.

Although additional research is necessary before these findings can be confidently generalized to other local government technologies, they suggest a number of implications for the future development of federal policy directed towards enhancing innovative activities in local governments.

First, there is a need for federal policy to consider the dynamics of local government resource allocation. Federal agencies dominant in each service sector should consider the status of their local counterparts vis-a-vis other local services in designing effective R&D strategies. Federal provision of technical assistance or training for local personnel, for example, may be inadequate stimuli for innovation in some local service sectors that face stiff competition from other local agencies in more advantageous political positions.

Second, the implications of this study are consistent with Yin, et al.'s suggestion that "federal support be undertaken with a capacity-building rather than case-specific objective" (1976: 155). We found that the nature of the impact of executive support for a specific technology is contingent upon the executive's organizational position. Thus, the net result of federal policies supportive of specific innovations may conceivably be to encourage local government officials to act at cross-purposes with one another. General approaches to increasing local government's capacity for change may be more fruitful. For instance, federal policies to increase the analytic and evaluative capacities of local governments may have more uniformly positive and predictable effects than support for specific technologies.

CONCLUSION

The results of two path analyses suggest that executive support is influential, not on the frequency of adoptions of computer applications, but on the distribution of adoptions among organizational subunits. The path model also indicates that increasing the levels of elected official and department head support actually constrains the widespread adoption of computer applications. This result suggests the possibility that computing innovations tend to be allocated in the same manner as existing resources, in accordance with executive perceptions of political advantage and need.

6 Determinants of Chief Executive Support*

In Chapter 5, attention was focused on the influences exerted on innovation outcomes by staffing and other organizational variables. In this analysis, attention is directed more closely to correlates of the judgmental components of executive support. Support is conceptualized as a predisposition grounded in an individual's cognitive and value judgments of the specific technology. Antecedents of these predispositions are analyzed to provide an indication of how different factors contribute to an executive's policy judgments.

In Chapter 5, we indicated that although there is some agreement on the importance of "overhead" influences in local government innovation processes, the chief executive's specific role is unclear. Beyond the questions regarding the determinants of those influences that we have discussed, the literature poses an additional set of questions. How is it that some studies indicate executives might be considerably involved and supportive of technological innovation, while other current studies indict the executives for lack of support? Is there anything about the character of the chief executives' support that warrants the frequent indictments linking the executives to innovation failures?

Two interrelated aspects of chief executive support pertinent to our

---

*This is a revised version of James L. Perry and Kenneth L. Kraemer, "The Chief Executive in Local Government Information Systems: Catalyst or Barrier to Innovation?," which appeared in Urban Systems, Vol. 2 (1977), pp. 121-131. It is reprinted by permission of Gordon A. Gebert, Editor, and Pergamon Press.

understanding of technological innovation in local governments are investigated in this study: 1) the concept of executive support for technological innovation; and 2) the correlates of the judgmental components of executive support for technological innovation.

The Concept of Executive Support

Studies which identify executive support as a determinant of innovation and implementation fall generally into two categories: 1) those that analyze the executive's supportiveness of technological innovations in which the activities of the role incumbent or position are the primary focus of the research (Dutton & Kraemer, 1978; Feller & Menzel, 1975; Radnor, Rubenstein & Tansik, 1970; Vertinsky & Barth, 1972; Yin, et al., 1976); and 2) those that analyze various dimensions of individual openness to change in which an individual's organizational position is treated as a secondary or unanalyzed variable in the research (Hage & Aiken, 1967; Mohr, 1969).

In these studies, executive support usually has been measured in one of two ways: 1) as the favorableness of beliefs or attitudes about a particular technology or set of technologies, or, more generally as openness to change; and 2) as observationally defined acts indicating commitment or the exercise of influence in efforts to incorporate technological innovations.

These conceptual and operational approaches to executive support have several shortcomings. Attitudinal studies, whether concerned with general or specific attitudes towards change, utilize a single attitudinal measure to operationalize the support concept (Mohr, 1969). In addition, studies which focus on general attitudes towards change, or on ideologies that would influence a specific type of innovation, tend to ignore the relationship between individual attributes and organizational attributes (Lin & Zaltman, 1973; Rogers, 1975). While behavioral studies can be expected to have a more direct linkage to innovation outcomes than the attitudinal studies, they have been unable to shed much light thus far on what motivates the executive's behavior. Furthermore, the measurement of executive behavior has not contributed significantly to an understanding of what types of behavior or what combinations of behaviors are instrumental in innovation adoption (Rogers, 1975).

CONCEPTUAL FRAMEWORK

In the present analysis, "support" is conceptualized as an outcome of two components of an individual's perceptions – current and expected utility. Current utility refers to the individual's perception of the current contribution of the technology as shaped by personal or "locally reported" experience with the technology. Expected utility refers to the individual's perception of the potential or future contribution of the technology as shaped by extrapolation of current experiences and by general images about the technology portrayed in the society. "Support" is conceptualized as the difference between an individual's perception of the expected utility of a technological innovation and an individual's perception of the current utility of the technology. The more positive the difference between the individual's perception of expected and current utility, the greater his support. The more negative the difference between the individual's perception of expected and current utility, the less his support.

This conceptualization treats support as a predisposition grounded in an individual's value and cognitive judgments of a specific technology or set of technologies (Kelman & Warwick, 1973; Schewe, 1976). It is a predisposition towards technology which depends on a positive relationship between future expected benefits from a technology and current, specific, identifiable benefits derived therefrom. Support, therefore, is highly rational; it is "given for returns." Support also is highly contingent; it varies more or less with successes and failures (Dennis, 1970; Dutton and Kraemer, 1978; Easton, 1965).

Our approach to the study of executive support can be understood by reference to an overall model of the relation between executive support and technological innovation shown in Fig. 15 (in italics). Moving left to right in the figure, technological innovation is viewed as a product of executive support and several intervening organizational factors such as the existence of slack resources and the kind of decision-making processes employed. Executive support itself is viewed as the outcome of two perceptual components: current and expected utility. These perceptions of utility held by executives, in turn, are viewed as related to several antecedents, particularly the current performance of the technology, the exeutive's contact with the technology, and environmental or organizational need/demand for the technology's use. In this context, then, we analyze the antecedents of the components of executive support as a basis for understanding more about the nature of executive support for technological innovation.

Analysis of the correlates of each of the perceptual components that influence the chief executive's predisposition towards technological innovation might provide an indication of how different factors contribute to a chief executive's policy judgments. What factors influence an individual's perceptions of the contribution of a technology? What factors influence an individual's expectations of a technology? Are these perceptions legitimate or are they based on misinformation or unrealistic expectations? Investigation of these questions should provide some insight into the probable appropriateness or inappropriateness of a chief executive's predisposition to support a technology. It also might lend insight into why the literature depicts chief executives as supportive of technological innovation and, at the same time, indicts them for implementation failures.

Data for the measures selected to examine these questions were derived from the URBIS survey of computing use, from the City and County Data Book 1972, (Appendix 1) and from U.S. Census reports.

Dependent Variables

The current and expected utility scales were derived from chief executive responses to the ten items in Table 24.(1) Based upon the arguments in the literature (Feller & Menzel, 1975; Mohr, 1969; Radnor, Rubenstein & Tansik,

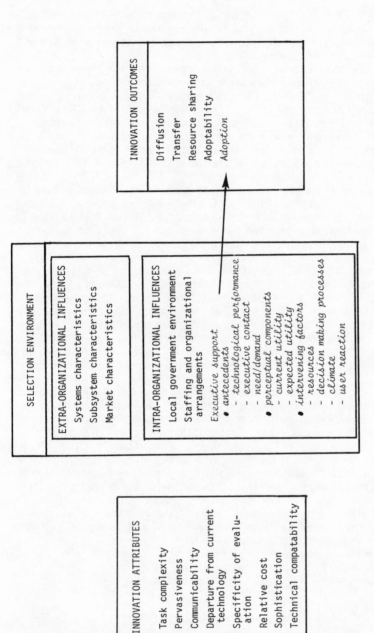

Figure 15. EXPANSION OF THE EXECUTIVE SUPPORT COMPONENT OF THE ANALYTIC MODEL[a]

[a]The variables in italics represent the specific portion of the
analytic model examined in this chapter.

1970), the support construct (i.e., the difference between expected utility and current utility) should predict critierion measures of technological innovation. Two measures of computing adoption were developed to test the criterion validity of the support construct. The number of computer applications in development was used to measure the frequency of innovation; the number of functions that have applications in development was used to measure the organizational scope of innovation.

Table 24. ITEMS USED IN DEVELOPING THE CURRENT AND EXPECTED UTILITY SCALES

Current Utility

Item

1. In general, computers provide information which is helpful to me in making decisions.

2. The computer makes information available to department heads that was not available before.

3. The computer is an essential tool in the day-to-day operations of this government.

4. Computing and data processing have generally failed to live up to my original expectations. (Reversed)

5. For the most part, computers have clearly increased the speed and ease of performance of government operations where they have been applied.

6. The use of computers and data processing results in greater co-operation among the operating departments and agencies.

7. I have indicated to department heads that computers and data processing should be used wherever economically feasible in this government.

Expected Utility

1. In the future, the computer will become much more essential in the day-to-day operations of this government.

2. In the future, a larger proportion of this local government's budget should support computers and data processing.

3. If properly designed and managed, much of the data gathered by this government in its daily operations could be collected and organized in ways that provide useful information about community conditions and government operations.

Independent Variables

Mohr (1969: 112), and other critical reviewers of existing innovation research (Downs & Mohr, 1976; Rogers, 1975; Warner, 1974), note that the empirical research on innovation employs "a strikingly heterogeneous selection of independent variables." The strategy in this study was to select variables which, on the basis of a priori judgment, could be expected to influence either a chief executive's perception of the technology's contribution or a chief executive's perception of its expected utility. Three types of variables were explored: technological performance, executive contact, and need/demand for the technology.

Technological performance is, in part, an elaboration of the concept of performance gaps. Rogers and Agarwala-Rogers (1976) define performance gaps as "perceptions of discrepancies between the organization's expectations and its actualities." Performance gaps have theoretically been treated as precursors of search behavior leading to organizational decisions to adopt innovations. However, when considering an innovation which is in some ways continuous, i.e., a new program similar to others implemented by an organization or a new computer application analogous to others adopted by an organization, the performance of these "technologies-in-practice" should influence the search and decision behavior of organizational members. In particular, we would expect the quality of technological performance to affect a chief executive's perception of the contribution of the technology and its expected utility.

The second set of factors which should influence perceptions is the amount of contact between the chief executive and the technology. An individual's use of a particular technology, for instance, might be an indication that the individual has some instrumental or sentimental attachment to the technology. For example, Swanson (1972) indicates that a manager's involvement with a management information system, either as a design participant or as an end user, produces appreciation of the system. The extent of an individual's familiarity with a technology also may be evidence of the individual's exposure to an environment which provides information supportive of the technology (Kelman & Warwick, 1973; Wynne & Dickson, 1975). We expect that use of a technology, or at least some familiarity with its capabilities, will be associated with perceptions of a technology's contribution and its expected utility.

The final hypothesized set of factors which potentially influence perceptions of a technology's current or expected utility are environmental and organizational definitions of need and demand for the technology. Rogers and Eveland (1976), Mohr (1969), Yin, et al. (1976), and Bingham (1975a) conclude that environmental and organizational pressures are critical factors in the local government innovation process. How these system attributes are translated into organizational action, however, is an unresolved issue in the literature. Bingham (1975a: 95) suggests that local government innovation is primarily a reflection of community and organizational political and social structures.

The community environment is directly related to policy adoptions in local government. The community environment is not directly related to bureaucratic innovation; however, the independent contributions to bureaucratic innovation beyond certain characteristics of the organization itself (e.g., size of the organization) are limited to responses to direct policy, and excess resources made available to the bureaucratic organization of the political system.

A less deterministic and possibly more accurate representation of the relationship between environmental and organizational factors and innovation would include the moderating influence of organizational member perceptions in the explanation. One of several linkages then between environmental and organizational variables and local government innovation would be through their effects on member attitudes and perception and, in turn, on member behavior in organizational decision making. Thus, we expect environmental and organizational definitions of need and demand for the technology to be associated with perceived contribution and expected utility.

Table 25 summarizes the specific variables used to measure each of the three sets of determinants discussed earlier. It also presents the expected relationships of these variables to chief executive perceptions. Implicit in our prediction of the relationships in Table 25 is our expectation that the relationships of the independent variables will be consistent across the two scales. We would expect, for example, that if operational performance is negatively associated with how the chief executive perceives the current utility of the technology, it will also be negatively associated with the chief executive's expectations of the future utility of the technology.

RESEARCH METHODOLOGY

Zero-order correlations were first computed between the innovation measures and support to test the validity of the support construct. Zero-order correlations were then computed between the current and expected utility scales and the antecedent variables. Additional partial correlations were computed using an index of information processing development as the control variable. Finally, the question of how well the three sets of variables predict chief executive perceptions was addressed through multiple regression analysis.

RESEARCH FINDINGS

Bivariate Analysis

The zero-order correlations between the innovation measures and support were .06 (nonsignificant) and .20 (significant at the .01 level), respectively. Thus, the results for the criterion validity of the support construct are mixed. Whether these results are a function of the nature of the chief executive's perceptions of current and expected utility is considered following an analysis of the antecedents of the components of the support construct.

The zero-order correlations between the current and expected utility scales and the three sets of antecedent variables are presented in Table 26.

Table 25. EXPECTATIONS ABOUT THE RELATIONSHIPS BETWEEN THE INDEPENDENT VARIABLES AND THE CURRENT AND EXPECTED UTILITY SCALES

Measurement	Independent Variable	Current Utility	Expected Utility
TECHNOLOGICAL PERFORMANCE			
Presence of "operational problems"--major foul-ups in day-to-day computing operations, unavailability of data for specific questions, late delivery of data processing products, difficulties in determining priorities, and getting and keeping qualified staff. (coefficient alpha = .59)	Operational Performance	−	−
Presence of "organizational problems"--proliferation of computer units, inadequate space for computing facilities and inappropriate department location of computing. (coefficient alpha = .50)	Organizational Problems	−	−
Presence of experienced data processing manager, personnel development programs, and positive rating of data processing management. (coefficient alpha = .68)	Personnel Performance	+	+
EXECUTIVE CONTACT			
Frequency of computer report use by chief executive, the executive's staff and the local legislative body. (coefficient alpha = .75)	Utilization of Computer Reports	+	+
Recency of chief executive's participation in a training course	Participation in a Training Course	+	+
NEED/DEMAND			
Organizational			
Cumulative presence of city manager form of administration, non-partisan elections, and at-large elections.	Reform	+	+
Use of professional management practices within legislative and administrative branches of government, including pay for councilmembers, staff aides for councilmembers, provision of services to council, use of written program objectives, and measures of performance use.	Professionalism	+	+
Size of the organizational work force servicing needs/demands.	Employees per Capita	+	+
Community			
Demographic heterogeniety - combines standardized scores for percent foreign, black, Catholic, and low income.	Social Diversity	−	−
Extent to which a multiplicity of groups are perceived by the chief executive as having influence in local decision making.	Pluralism	+	+
Size of community population generating needs/demands	Log of Population	+	+

The predictions about the relationships of technological performance to chief executive perceptions are generally supported by the results for the current utility scale, but unsupported for the expected utility scale. Personnel performance has no significant relationship with either scale. Operational performance, the measure most closely associated with the actual performance of the technology, has the strongest association with current utility. Operational performance, however, has no association with expected utility. Utilization of computer-generated reports is positively and significantly associated with both scales. The results for the need/demand variables, unlike the results for the two sets of variables associated directly with the technology, are much less in accord with our expectations. The direction of the relationships for reform are opposite those we anticipated and, in one instance, are significant. Administrative professionalism is positively and significantly associated with both current and expected utility. Employees per capita and pluralism are significant.

Table 26. ZERO-ORDER CORRELATIONS BETWEEN THE ANTECEDENT VARIABLES AND THE CURRENT AND EXPECTED UTILITY SCALES

	Current Utility		Expected Utility	
	r	(N)	r	(N)
Technological Performance				
Operational performance	-.29***	(479	.00	(481)
Organizational problems	-.10*	(474)	.00	(475)
Personnel performance	.06	(348)	.03	(350)
Executive Contact				
Utilization of computer reports	.40***	(503)	.18***	(503)
Participation in training course	.03	(500)	.07	(500)
Need/Demand				
Organizational				
Reform	-.07*	(555)	-.01	(559)
Professionalism	.10**	(551)	.08*	(555)
Employees/capita	.06	(544)	.03	(549)
Community				
Social diversity	-.06	(541)	-.02	(545)
Pluralism	.12**	(542)	.15***	(544)
Log of population	.02	(555)	.00	(559)

$*$ a < .05
$**$ a < .01
$***$ a < .001

Controlling for Development Status

As noted earlier, attitudinal studies of support tend to ignore the relationship between individual attributes and organizational attributes and, thus, the contextual situation of an adopter unit with respect to the focal innovation or innovations. This raises an issue of whether the significant relationships between the technological performance and executive contact variables and chief executive perceptions may be spurious or, alternatively, whether they reflect the state of development of computing within the organization.   Three alternative possibilities for the relationships among development status, the technology-related indicators, and the contribution of EDP as perceived by the chief executives are diagrammed in Fig. 16.

To measure the level of EDP development, a scale was created based upon the presence or absence of five information processing tasks in the local government organization. The five information processing tasks are: record-keeping, calculating/printing, record restructuring, sophisticated analytics, and process control (Danziger, 1977; Kraemer, Dutton & Matthews, 1975). These information processing tasks are theoretically indicative of a progression from minor to major restructuring of the information flows within the organization. Wynne and Dickson (1975: 26) summarize this progression:

1. Most organizations simply automate their existing information flows.

2. Some firms first revise their information flows and then automate these modernized processes.

3. A very few firms act upon the answer to questions such as: "What should be done differently?" and "What operations are newly feasible, given the powers of the computer?"

The five different information processing tasks were used to construct an index of information processing development by Guttman scaling. Cutpoints for the scale were based on the following criteria: 1) local governments with no more than one application in any of the categories; 2) two or more applications in the calculating/printing or calculating/printing and record-keeping categories; 3) two or more applications in the preceding two categories as well as record restructuring and sophisticated analytics; and 4) two or more applications in each of the five information processing categories.   The coefficient of reproducibility for the development status scale is .93.

Partial correlations, using development status as the control variable, were computed between the technological performance and executive contact variables and current utility scale to test for the relationships presented in Fig. 16. The partial correlations for the operational performance, organizational problems, and utilization of computer reports relationships remained relatively unchanged with coefficients of -.31, -.11, and .39, respectively. This result suggests that the developmental sequence depicted in Fig. 16(a) is a good representation of the relationships among development status, the technology-related indicators, and the current utility of the technology as perceived by the chief executive.

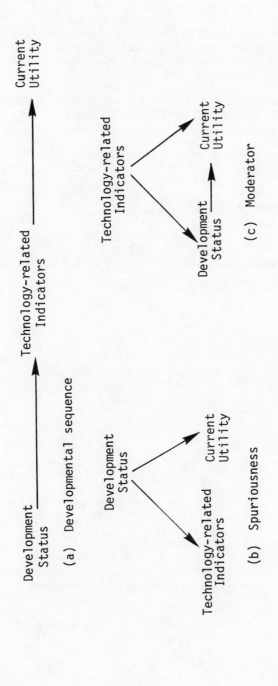

Figure 16. ALTERNATIVE MODELS OF THE RELATIONSHIPS AMONG DEVELOPMENT STATUS, THE TECHNOLOGY-RELATED INDICATORS AND CURRENT UTILITY

Multiple Regression Analysis

Results of the regression analysis for each scale are presented in Table 27. The regression equation for current utility achieves overall significance, but the prediction equation for expected utility is nonsignificant.

Table 27.   MULTIPLE REGRESSION RESULTS FOR THE INDEPENDENT VARIABLES AND THE CURRENT AND EXPECTED UTILITY SCALES

	Current Utility	Expected Utility
Technological Performance		
Operational performance	-.25***	-.06
Organizational problems	-.12**	.00
Personnel performance	.03	.00
Executive Contact		
Utilization of computer reports	.35***	.16***
Participation in training course	.10*	.09
Need/Demand		
Organizational		
Reform	-.08	.00
Professionalism	.06	.10*
Employees/capita	.00	.10
Community		
Social Diversity	-.05	-.10*
Pluralism	.06	.06
Population, logged	.04	-.04
Constant	1.41	.82
R^2	.27	.07
F	9.47***	2.06

* p < .05
** p < .01
*** p < .001

DISCUSSION

These results raise a serious question about the probable influence of chief executive support for local government computing. Is support the rationale, contingent phenomenon we conceptualized, or, is it nonrational or irrational? The findings indicate that the executives' perceptions of the current utility of computing are grounded in the assessment of a number of technology-specific factors — operational performance, organizational problems, utilization of computer reports. These variables related as expected to the chief executive's perception of the current utility of computing to local government activities. These relationships still hold when the development status of the technology in the organization is considered.

However, the influence of technological performance and executive contact is reflected only selectively in the chief executive's expected utility for computing. Utilization of computer reports is positively and uniformly associated with both the current and expected utility scales. The significant negative relationships of operational performance and organizational problems to current utility, however, are not reflected in the correlations for the chief executive's expected utility. Executives who currently perceive benefits from computing along with technological and organizational problems also expect future benefits from computing, but without the technological and organizational problems.

This tendency of chief executives to anticipate future benefits from computing without the attendant problems is clearly an instance of selective perception resulting in unrealistic expectations. It suggests that some chief executives support computing innovation because they overlook the problems attendant to the technology's use. This finding might explain why there are so many failures in the implementation of computing technology in local governments and other organizations. Some executives might be giving misplaced and uncritical support to technological innovation, thereby encouraging unnecessary, counterproductive, or overly-expensive innovations.

However, there is also another explanation for the selective perception, and it, too, probably characterizes some of the executives. The consistent positive relationship between top management utilization of computer reports and both current and expected utility suggests that the executives may value personal benefits more than organizational disbenefits. Computing apparently produces organizational disbenefits in the form of poor operational performance and multiple organizational problems. But, computing apparently also provides the executives with reports useful to them in decision making; and current EDP promotional efforts probably lead them to expect even more information/decision benefits in the future. Therefore, executives who get such information and have low organizational disbenefits probably expect more of the same. However, executives who now get such information and have high organizational disbenefits probably discount the problems as normal, or as offset by the value of getting information they want. This suggests that the executives might be paying little attention to the broader benefits and costs of data processing so long as they get personal benefits. This is clearly suboptimization which might have high costs to the organization and might increase the possibility for failures.

From a policy perspective, this assessment, together with the relationship between chief executive support and scope of local government computer application adoption, suggests that at least a portion of computing innovation in local government might be unnecessary and possibly counterproductive. Some chief executives, either because they are unrealistic about the problems with computing or because they suboptimize for personal gain, lend uncritical support to computing adoptions. If problems and failures are to be avoided, they would do well to critically examine each proposed new computing application for its own merit and for its fit with the organization's needs.

CONCLUSION

The results of this analysis indicate that reported failures to achieve the potential of urban management technologies may be as much the result of executive support as the result of a lack of support. The unpredictability of executive expectations about the utility of computing clearly demonstrates a need for assessing how local government decision makers approach technological decisions which require long lead times. Poorly conceived adoptions of management technologies can multiply impediments to local government innovation created by negative user reactions and organizational inertia.

III
Research Findings

7 Assessment of Diffusion and Adoption

The preceding chapters have explored various aspects of computer application diffusion and adoption in U.S. local governments. This chapter summarizes the findings of our analyses.

DIFFUSION OF COMPUTER APPLICATIONS AMONG LOCAL GOVERNMENTS

The Influence of Innovation Attributes and Policy Interventions on the Diffusion of Computer Applications

The diffusion patterns of computer applications among local governments were found to be highly diverse. Rather than uncovering a uniform S-shaped pattern for the applications we studied, we found a diverse set of diffusion patterns ranging from the typical cumulative normal distribution (S-shaped curve) to reasonably flat cumulative distributions, indicative of applications that were subject to several early adoptions but which subsequently were unadopted.

We found in two different analyses that diffusion patterns were significantly related to innovation attributes and to policy interventions. In the first, we used unidimensional (extent and rate of adoption) outcome measures to assess the relationships of innovation attributes and policy interventions to the diffusion of computer applications. Multiple regressions for the unidimensional outcome measures revealed that three innovation attributes were generally significant predictors of diffusion: departure from current technologies, pervasiveness, and specificity of evaluation. The extent to which an application departed from those technologies currently used by local governments had a positive impact on the subsequent number of adoptions, but negatively influenced the initial rate of adoption. The pervasiveness or organization-wide utility of applications, such as those in the

119

finance function, also were more highly valued candidates for automation than were applications with less pervasive implications. Increasing ability to objectively assess the outputs of an application was likewise positively related to extent and rate of adoption.

The policy variables fared less well than innovation attributes in the multiple regressional analysis. Professional communication was a weak predictor of both extent and rate of adoption. Federal financial assistance was a significant positive determinant of the initial rate of adoption. A plausible reason for the weak relationships of the policy variables in the regressions is possible interaction between the policy interventions and the innovation attributes. If such interaction exists, the regressions would have understated the contribution of the policy variables to diffusion of computer applications. Although we tested for interaction effects among these two sets of variables, we were unable to identify any.

In the second analysis, we used a multidimensional outcome measure to assess the ability of the innovation attributes and policy variables to differentiate among diffusion patterns. The population of 255 computer applications was grouped according to similarities in their overall pattern of diffusion forming nine different diffusion groups. Discriminant analysis of the innovation attributes and policy variables indicated that the diffusion of computer applications among local governments is facilitated by system characteristics and by the attributes of the application. The systemic factors which facilitated diffusion were the departure of the application from other technologies in use and the availability of federal resources for designing and implementing the application. Three application attributes were about equally significant in facilitating diffusion: pervasiveness, departure from existing technologies, and specificity of evaluation. Thus, the results of both analyses were mutually reinforcing.

The results of the multiple regression and discriminant analyses also suggested that several processes underlie computer application diffusion among local governments. One process was described as need-based in which felt needs, search, and adoption by some system members (local governments) lead to subsequent diffusion to others with similar felt needs. Alternative causal processes also were supported by the analysis. Among the alternative processes was the incentive value of federal funding for encouraging local officials to adopt new applications.

The Influence of Cooperation in Urban Intergovernmental Networks on Diffusion Transfer

As a complement to our analysis of computer application diffusion among local governments nationally, we also explored diffusion within a major type of local government subsystem, Standard Metropolitan Statistical Areas. The SMSA was treated conceptually as a network in which cooperation among local governments was defined in terms of 1) rate of diffusion, 2) amount of application transfer activity, and 3) the extent of consolidated use of computing facilities, equipment, and personnel. For each of these forms of cooperation, we explored the association with relational or environmental properties of urban intergovernmental networks.

The results moderately supported the proposition that characteristics of the urban intergovernmental network influence the rate of diffusion of computer applications. The factors which were significant in explaining variance in the rate of diffusion were highly diverse across the four applications considered in the analysis. Supplier availability and LEAA funding contributed to the diffusion of the police service data application. The levels of HUD and LEAA funding, however, were negatively associated with the diffusion of real property records applications within urban networks. Participation in URISA conferences had a significant influence on the intergovernmental diffusion of revenue forecasting applications. On the other hand, the level of partisanship among SMSA cities was negatively associated with the diffusion of the budget preparation application.

The transfer of applications within urban intergovernmental networks was associated with variables distinguishable from those important in predicting diffusion. Three variables accounted for a significant portion of the variance in transfers: 1) the SMSA mean for vendor programming of applications, 2) the SMSA mean level of slack resources, and 3) the SMSA mean level of revenue sharing funds. Several possible causal relationships could be responsible for the findings, but the results cannot be considered conclusive. The negative relationship of vendor programming suggests that vendor programmed applications are difficult to transfer to other local government contexts. It is likely that in order to maintain their markets, external suppliers would design software for local governments that makes transfer to other equipment difficult. The positive and significant relationships for both revenue sharing funding and slack resources suggested the need for the availability of considerable resource flexibility before transfers can occur. Only URISA membership was statistically significant in the resource sharing regression. We suggest low concentrations of professionals or "cosmopolitans" may serve as a centripetal force, motivating resource pooling among local governments. In contrast, substantial concentrations of professionals might have a greater interest in the autonomy of their organization's computing resources, thus creating a centrifugal force within the network.

The Influence of Market Variables on the Transfer of Computer Applications

An assessment of four key points in the literature about computerized information systems indicates application transfer is a logical idea and potentially could provide substantial benefits. However, the experience of cities and counties shows that frequently something goes wrong.

The reasons for the failure or infeasibility of application transfer are numerous. Contrary to popular belief, the best candidate to undertake transfer may be the governments with highly developed EDP systems. They (and probably few other local governments) are capable of undertaking the complexities of independent search, evaluation, and transfer. Furthermore, computer applications can seldom be transferred and adapted for only a "small fraction" of the time and money needed to develop them in-house. Unfortunately, it is common for any or all of a host of technical problems to occur, and, in reality, substantial savings occur only under the best of conditions.

ADOPTION OF COMPUTER APPLICATIONS
BY LOCAL GOVERNMENTS

Environmental Determinants of the
Adoptability of Computer Applications

Although the analyses of computer application diffusion led to several significant findings, we were also interested in developing a more precise understanding of the adoption decision in local governments. Our focus was the adoptability of computer organizations by local governments. What makes one application more likely to be adopted than another?

We employed four broad conceptual dimensions in our analysis of adoptability: 1) relation of the innovation to organizational domain, 2) integration, 3) risk, and 4) need. These dimensions encompassed many of the more concrete variables considered in previous studies of local government innovation adoption and minimized the problem of complex interaction among the variables. An innovation-decision design, which employs an innovation in relation to an organization as the unit of analysis, was used in the empirical study.

For the most part, the results did not support the explicit operational relationships we hypothesized for the relationships between the four conceptual dimensions and adoptability. The results, however, did indicate that four dimensions had significant influences on adoptability and that the effects of the variables were frequently non-linear. Five components of the conceptual dimensions made significant independent contributions to the explanation of variance in application adoption: task-maintenance orientation of the innovation, visibility of the innovation, supplier availability, uncertainty, and need. Among these five variables, linear relationships were supported only for the visibility and supplier availability variables.

The most striking results were derived from our analysis of interactions among the four conceptual dimensions we measured. This analysis suggested some interesting dynamics:

1. Staff competence, visibility of an innovation, and supplier proximity are more critical to adoption when an application relates to task accomplishment rather than maintenance aspects of an organization's domain.

2. Risk has almost no influence on adoptability when an application is task-oriented, but becomes the major determinant of adoptability when an application is maintenance-oriented.

3. Risk also accounts for a substantially greater portion of the variance in adoption when integration is high than when integration is low.

4. For adoption decisions which involve minimal risks, the controlling factors in the adoption decision become whether an application is task-oriented or maintenance-oriented and whether or not the organization is integrated with suppliers and external technological developments.

5. Staff competence, the innovation's visibility, and supplier proximity are likely to create some pressures for adoption even in the absence of need.

Staffing and Organizational Influence on Computer Application Adoption

A direct test of whether chief executive support does indeed influence the adoption of computer applications revealed a weak positive relationship with only one of two outcome measures. A distinction was made between two innovation outcomes: 1) the magnitude of innovation, i.e., the number of applications adopted, and 2) the scope of innovation, i.e., the number of subunits automating. The results of two path analyses suggested that executive support is influential, not in the frequency of computer application adoption, but in the distribution of adoptions among organizational subunits. The path model for innovation scope also indicated that increasing the levels of elected official and department head support of computing actually constrains the widespread adoption of computer applications. This result suggests the possible tendency for computing innovations to reinforce and strengthen existing patterns of resource allocation. Elected officials are likely to allocate resources for computing to organizational subunits differentially just as they allocate resources for other goods and services, in accordance with their perceptions of political advantage or need. Widespread department head support for computing also guarantees that previously successful bureaucratic entrepreneurs have a greater likelihood of claiming new resources.

Determinants of Chief Executive Support for Computer Application Adoption

As an additional step in assessing the influence of the chief executive upon computer application adoption by local governments, we developed a construct of support and analyzed its correlates. Support was conceptualized as the difference between two measures of individual perceptions of benefits from computing. The first measure, expected utility, represents expectations about future benefits from computing. Current utility represents perceptions of current benefits derived from computing.

An analysis of the correlates of these two measures revealed that the chief executive's perception of the current utility of computing was grounded in the assessment of three technology-specific factors: operational performance, organizational problems, and utilization of computer reports. Expected utility, on the other hand, was related to few of the correlates we studied. It was apparent from the analysis that some executives who currently perceive benefits from computing as well as technological and organizational problems also expect future benefits from computing, but without the technological and organizational problems. The results suggest that some chief executives support computing innovation because they overlook the problems attendant to the technology's use. Some executives might be giving misplaced and uncritical support to computing, thereby encouraging unnecessary, counterproductive, or overly-expensive innovations which fail as a result of their ill-conception.

CONCLUSION

Our examination of the processes of technological innovation in American local governments has been guided by an analytic model composed of three categories of variables: innovation attributes, selection environment, and innovation outcomes. In each chapter we explicated and tested relationships among variables associated with different parts of the analytic model. Although the analyses of the model were piecemeal, they suggest several directions for building a general theory of technological innovation in local government as well as some of the difficulties associated with such an enterprise. This discussion of the model is focused around two issues: 1) the substance and structure of the model, and 2) methodological considerations.

The Substance and Structure of the Model

The analytic model we first presented in Chapter 1 associated three primary clusters of variables with innovation outcomes. The three clusters were labeled innovation attributes, extra-organizational influences and intra-organizational influences. In at least one significant respect – the inclusion of innovation attributes – this model differs from others which have traditionally been used to study technological innovation in local governments.

Each cluster of variables proved to contain significant contributors to one or more of the innovation outcomes we investigated. While the significance of individual variables is important information in terms of our understanding of innovation, an issue more pertinent to the overall worth of the model, however, is that of the contribution of each major set of explanatory variables. How significant are the relative contributions of innovation attributes, extra-organizational influences and intra-organizational influences to innovation outcomes? Our investigation provides no easy answer to that question. The innovation attributes proved to be good predictors of diffusion patterns; and in conjunction with some organizational attributes the innovation attributes were also good predictors of adoptability. These findings suggest that innovation attributes should be included in future efforts to explain and model technological innovation, but they do not indicate whether innovation attributes in the aggregate explain a lessor or greater share of the variance in innovation outcomes than, for instance, intra-organizational influences.

The results suggest that innovation attributes and systems, market, and organizational characteristics may be a great deal more significant than subsystems or individual variables. This represents one plausible weighting of the contributions of the variables which might be investigated in the future.

An issue related to the relative contributions of the clusters of variables is that of the complexity of the technological innovation process itself. Our results suggest that the process is as complex – and perhaps more – as the analytic model we presented in the course of this book. The sources of variance in innovation outcomes are considerable. More important, our examination of technological innovation in local government suggests that innovation is a highly contingent phenomenon. This affirms the earlier results of Mohr (1969) and Downs (1976). Researchers in the future must employ analytic models which recognize the contingent nature of the phenomena as well as the frequently non-linear functional forms of the relationships.

Methodological Considerations

Two general methodological points are worthy of emphasis in this assessment of the technological innovation model. The first concerns the cumulativeness of innovation research findings and the seocnd concerns the range of outcome variables.

Research on innovation has recently been criticized because of the non-cumulative findings (Downs & Mohr, 1976). This book has presented a series of analyses which are cumulative in at least two respects. First, the analyses have employed a single analytic model and therefore each chapter has served both to check and to reinforce findings of other chapters. Second, since we have looked at a single technology, computing, each analysis has served to deepen our understanding of the innovation processes surrounding that technology.

Future research must strive to be more cumulative by recognizing the linkages among the different levels of analysis (e.g., the individual, the organization, and the system) and among different units of analysis (e.g., diffusion, transfer, and adoption). Studies of the adoption of innovations by organizations must include variables which measure variations in the external system. Studies of individual innovative behavior must consider the "situation" or "context" of that behavior. In the absence of research linking together these different levels of analysis, innovation research will continue to be non-cumulative.

As a counterpoint to the need for greater integration among studies at different levels of analysis is a need for diversity in the definition of researchable innovation outcomes. We have used a number of outcome variables for the purpose of exploring different facets of innovation. As the cumulative results of our investigation indicate, this type of multiple outcome analysis is necessary from a practical and also a theoretical perspective. In the past, however, researchers have been too willing to discard several measures in deference to a single "appropriate" measure. Using several measures should provide a check on results across measures and assure that distinctions among different types of innovative activity do not go uninvestigated in the future.

8 Assessment of Federal Policy

In this final chapter, we assess the impacts and effectiveness of federal policy for the transfer of computer applications to local governments and suggest several options for improving federal policy. First, we identify some of the policy relevant findings about diffusion processes that our analyses have provided. Then, we assess the match between these processes and federal policy toward the development of computing. Finally, we conclude with suggestions for future federal policy and research.

Chapter 7 described our research findings about application diffusion and adoption processes. We now isolate several of these findings that hold particular relevance for our examination of the fit between federal policy and processes for the diffusion of computer applications to local government.

POLICY RELEVANT FINDINGS ABOUT THE DIFFUSION OF APPLICATIONS AMONG LOCAL GOVERNMENTS

The Design of an Application Has a Significant Influence on its Subsequent Diffusion

We found that diffusion was enhanced for applications with organization-wide utility, outputs that could be specified and evaluated, and an orientation towards both task and maintenance objectives of the local government. For example, financial management applications are likely candidates for adoption because they are linked to operations within all local government subunits; their performance can be relatively easily compared with both traditional non-automated procedures and explicit evaluative criteria; and they contribute both to resource control and to resource allocation among the services provided by local governments. In contrast, client information and referral systems are much less likely to be adopted since they are linked to services provided mainly outside the government, confined to use within a single local agency, difficult to evaluate for possible adoption, and oriented primarily toward assisting clients to make their way through the service systems.

The Supply and Demand Side of the Local Government Computer Application Market Function Quite Effectively and Do Not Appear to be Major Impediments to Diffusion

We base our conclusion about the supply side of the market on an investigation of the effects of the availability of software suppliers (e.g., private firms, federal and state agencies) on both the rate of diffusion of applications within SMSAs and the decision by individual local governments to adopt a particular application. The number of local suppliers of computing software had no influence on innovation diffusion or adoptability. Local governments either have local access to a sufficient number of suppliers, or, if the supply side of the local market is inadequate, local governments can draw upon regional or national suppliers outside of their geographic area.

On the demand side, the major issue we investigated was diversity in the local government computer applications market. The diversity of local governments is considered to be a major barrier to creating profitable markets for software suppliers. We found that the diversity of local governments is neither significantly different from that of the private sector nor as substantial as the literature suggests. Characteristics such as size and wealth, which on the basis of private sector studies might be expected to reflect the diversity of the local applications market, were significantly related to diffusion patterns. However, among all the characteristics studied, size (reflecting the volume of information processing) and wealth (reflecting the probable breadth of services) were the only characteristics of adopters which differentiated applications classified according to their extent and rate of adoption.

Other characteristics often assumed to be associated with diversity unique to the local government market were non-significant. Characteristics such as the percentage of intergovernmental revenue, whether the governmental unit was a city or county, and the region in which the local government was located were poor predictors of variations in diffusion patterns. Thus, diversity in the local government market is related to factors similar to those in the private sector, but not to factors unique to local governments.

System Building Is an Incremental Rather Than a Comprehensive Process

Local government information systems might be constructed through comprehensive system-building efforts or might evolve through incremental development. Comprehensive information systems, such as FAMIS (Financial Accounting and Management Information Systems)(1) and PROMIS (Prosecution Management Information System), were predicted as not likely to be widely adopted by local governments. However, independent applications which performed some functions of these comprehensive systems were (or were likely to be) widely adopted. Collectively, independent applications frequently perform many of the same functions as the comprehensive systems. While we were unable to determine whether the resulting aggregate of applications are qualitatively equivalent to the comprehensive systems, it seems clear that systems performing similar tasks eventually result from the two avenues of incorporation. Furthermore, the development of computing is more likely to proceed incrementally than comprehensively because of the difficulty of rapid and simultaneous acquisition of fiscal resources, in-house expertise, high level hardware capability, and organizational member acceptance of sophisticated uses of computing.

Some Applications Are More Critical Than Others in Overall Development of Local Government Automated Information Systems Because of Their "Gateway" Capacity

The gateway capacity of an innovation refers to the idea that "in addition to the intrinsic value derived from the adoption of an innovation, value may accrue to the extent that the <u>adoption of an innovation may open avenues to the adoption of other innovation</u>"(emphasis in original). (2) This idea is particularly applicable to innovations which are in some ways continuous, such as computer applications. It is entirely reasonable that some computer applications would provide the foundation for other subsequent applications. In a number of instances, we found the diffusion of an application was considerably greater than what was expected due simply to its characteristics. For example, several police and property assessment applications diffused much more rapidly and extensively than expected. We believe this attributable to the gateway capacity of basic police and assessment applications. The Census Bureau's Address Coding Guide (ACG) application appears to be similarly related to the diffusion and adoption of DIME, ADMATCH, GRIDS, CUE and other geoprocessing applications.

The Experiences of Local Governments Show That Transfer Is Infrequently Relied Upon as a Means of Application Acquisition and, When it is Used, Something Frequently Goes Wrong(3)

Despite the widespread adoption of computing by local governments, few inter-jurisdictional transfers have taken place. The commonly asserted benefits of transfer such as low developmental costs and time savings for implementation are seldom realizable. In fact, our results suggest that transfer occurs most readily with resource flexibility rather than resource constraints. For smaller local governments just beginning to automate their tasks, a combination of vendors and in-house personnel appears adequate for meeting their needs. Transfer becomes an efficient means of application acquisition only for larger, experienced local governments in search of relatively unique, specialized applications. Even then, our findings suggest that a considerable amount of slack resources will have to be available in both the transferor and transferee organizations for transfer to be a viable means for acquisition of an application.

Federal Financial Support Is a Significant Facilitator of Application Diffusion but, on Balance, its Contribution to Local Development Might Be Marginal

This finding is supported by other recent research which indicates that incentives increase the extent and rate of adoption of an innovation; but the quality of adoption decisions may be relatively low, leading to undesired or unintended consequences.(4) Our analysis indicates that adoption decisions motivated by federal financial support tend to overlook more beneficial applications for which there is no support, and also tend to overlook the inadequacy of federally supported applications in meeting local government needs. Our results further indicate that even in the absence of federal assistance, applications with attributes attractive to local governments probably will diffuse widely and relatively quickly. For example, we indicated earlier that financial management applications diffuse widely without federal support. Moreover, our analysis suggests that federal assistance might distort local development priorities. We found that LEAA (Law Enforcement Assistance Administration) assistance was positively related to diffusion of police applications within SMSAs, but negatively related (rather than unrelated) to diffusion of non-police applications. These results suggest that functionally oriented federal assistance shifts resource utilization not only in the supported department of the local government, but also shifts resources away from automation in other functional departments. Apparently the federal assistance changes local development priorities because the local government's development capacity is limited at any one time.

FEDERAL POLICY AND THE DIFFUSION OF COMPUTER APPLICATIONS AMONG LOCAL GOVERNMENTS: CONVERGENCE OR DIVERGENCE?

In considering the relationship between the dimensions of federal policy for the computer applications to local governments and the empirically based conclusions about application diffusion and adoption among local governments, two topics merit attention: 1) the effectiveness of federal design approaches and transfer mechanisms when judged against the diffusion criterion, and 2) the effectiveness of federal policies when judged by their "fit" with the processes associated with diffusion of applications among local governments. Federal policies, design approaches, and transfer mechanisms were presented earlier in the Introduction and are summarized in Fig. 17.

Only one design approach and a single transfer mechanism enjoy significant success when judged against the diffusion criterion. The functional approach to software design, with its reliance on a federal agency developing a range of applications for its local government counterpart, has been much more successful than either the comprehensive or the ad hoc design

approaches. Similarly, federal subsidy has achieved a much greater diffusion
effect than research and demonstration or programmatic requirements.

The reasons for the different levels of effectiveness of the federal design
and transfer approaches are apparent from the findings of our studies. The
functional design approach is more likely to take account of local needs

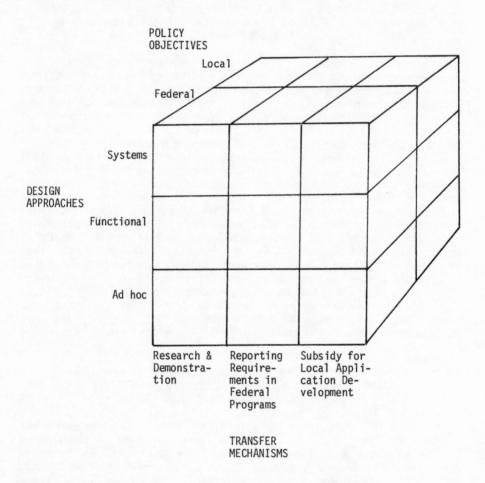

Figure 17.   RELATED DIMENSIONS OF FEDERAL POLICY FOR
COMPUTER TECHNOLOGY TRANSFER

because of the strong ties between the federal agency and its local counterpart.   Similarly, the range of applications and long-term federal agency commitment typically associated with the functional approach improve the visibility of applications, enhance incremental system-building processes at the local level, and produce "leader" (gateway) as well as "follower" applications. Both the comprehensive and ad hoc design approaches have shortcoming in one of these areas. Comprehensive designs are inconsistent with incremental system-building processes and can be expected to tax local data processing expertise. Ad hoc design approaches, while more closely related to the functional approach than the comprehensive approach, fail to take account of the gateway effects of some applications and are likely to produce less visible applications.

A similar assessment can be made of the three mechanisms for transfer of computer applications. Research and demonstration, with its assumption that advanced prototypes will diffuse widely once built, is inadequate as a transfer mechanism on two grounds. Very little transfer of applications occurs by comparison to the amount of in-house development of applications in local governments.(5) And, common assertions about the ease, speed, cost savings and other benefits of transfer seldom fit the reality of transfer experiences in local governments.

Reporting requirements in federal programs tend to induce rapid adoption initially, but are unsuccessful in the long run. Since federal reporting requirements seldom are compatible with local information requirements, the automated reporting systems are ultimately incompatible with local goals. Consequently, the local governments discontinue the systems when federal programs support ends.(6) This is both a failure to recognize incompatibilities between federal and local information needs and a failure to recognize where those needs might be compatible.

Subsidy, though it has accomplished diffusion, also is doubtful as a transfer mechanism because it can be cost ineffective and lead to unpredictable consequences. It is cost ineffective when the local governments use federal funds to adopt systems they would have adopted without the federal support.   Federal subsidy sometimes merely displaces rather than supplements local funds, and therefore does not act as a necessary condition for the adoption of computer applications.(7) Subsidy also tends to be a relatively unpredictable transfer mechanism because there are few constraints on what kinds of computer applications the local agencies may develop. Subsidy seems well suited for building local computing capability and for reinforcing local automation goals, but these may have little to do with federal goals.

A POLICY IMPLICATIONS

A number of policy implications can be drawn from the results of this analysis.

The Role of Federal Support

Federal financial assistance is an effective intervention for the diffusion of computer applications. Federal assistance is likely to be most successful when it is directed towards applications which represent a breakthrough from technologies in use and which possess attributes attractive to local governments. The findings are far from unambiguous, however, in indicating that federal assistance is necessary, or necessarily desirable. Even in the absence of federal assistance, applications with attributes attractive to local governments can be expected to diffuse widely and relatively quickly. Furthermore, our analysis of diffusion rates in SMSAs suggests that federal assistance might distort local development priorities by increasing the speed of development of supported versus non-supported applications.

Given some of these caveats, thorough analysis of the local government market for computer applications would appear to be a prerequisite for developing a program of federal support. Such analysis must explore local needs for new uses of the computer, local responsiveness to particular types of computing innovations, and the ways in which current local government uses of the computer are deficient. Where federal and local objectives for incorporation of an application are in agreement, the publication and wide distribution of information about local markets and needs by the federal government might itself be adequate support for the "take-off" and subsequent extensive diffusion of certain applications. Our discriminant analysis of the characteristics of adopters indicated that – with the exception of two measures of size (population and expenditures) – no characteristics were able to account for segmentation of the local government computer application market. Indeed, there might be less segmentation within the local government market than previously thought. The major impediment to the improvement of local government technologies might be the inefficiency of mechanisms for conveying information about the local government market to potential suppliers.

Federal Strategies for Involvement

Our analysis suggests that present federal design approaches and transfer mechanisms for the diffusion of applications are not particularly effective. One reason is the failure of federal agencies to give sufficient recognition to the differences in federal and local information needs and the nature of automated systems required to meet these needs, either simultaneously in a single system or through separate systems. Another reason is the tendency of federal agencies to consider the various design approaches and transfer mechanisms as mutually exclusive, and therefore, to fail to consider policy options which mix the design approaches and the transfer mechanisms. Two options that merit consideration are consistent with our research.

First, where federal objectives for the development of a new application differ from local objectives, a two-stage program of federal support might be the most effective strategy for intervention. The first stage would provide general subsidies for the development of local capabilities in areas related to the targeted application. The second stage would then be directed at programmatic requirements to encourage the adoption of federally-targeted applications.

Second, it is important that federal strategies recognize the incremental pattern of automation development in local governments. Generally, locally developed systems are built in increments which evolve, through redevelopment, towards more integrated, comprehensive and sophisticated applications. Consequently, an effective federal strategy for intervention might be to mold incrementally the direction of local development through the provision of sequenced sets of applications each of which builds upon previously established capacities. Of course, this requires continuous and sustained, though not necessarily large, federal support for application diffusion.

Role of Professional Associations

Our analyses of diffusion both among local governments nationally and within SMSAs indicated that professional communication channels and professional associations which were "computing-specific" made minimal independent contributions to the diffusion of applications. On the other hand, more general organizational properties of local governments such as staff competence and professionalism did contribute to the adoptability of applications and to the magnitude and scope of organizational innovation. These results suggest that an organization's general norms and its capacity to use an innovation are critical parameters of the policy calculus for improving local government technology.

Application Transfer

Transfer does not appear to be an efficient means for the diffusion of applications among all local governments. For smaller local governments just beginning to automate their tasks, a combination of vendors and in-house personnel appears adequate for meeting their needs. Transfer becomes an efficient means of application acquisition only for larger, experienced local governments in search of relatively unique, specialized applications. Even then, our findings suggest that a considerable amount of slack resources will have to be available in both organizations for transfer to be a viable means for acquisition of an application.

Enhancing Local Evaluative Capabilities

Several of our findings point to the need for improving the analytic capabilities of local governments for evaluating computer applications being considered for adoption. Improving local governments' capacity to evaluate the contributions of specific applications should reduce the uncertainty surrounding new applications and increase their adoptability. Disseminating objective evaluations (by outsiders) of the experience of technological leaders to other local governments also might be helpful for developing realistic expectations among local government officials.

The Politics of Innovation Adoption

Several of our findings indicate that adoption of innovations is a political activity rather than the apolitical process most frequently portrayed in the diffusion literature. Which computer applications are adopted is determined in large part by existing patterns of power, influence, and resource allocation in local governments. Those government functions which already have computing innovations, which already have other innovations, and which tend to receive the larger share of local resources also tend to have a greater likelihood of getting computer applications adopted in their area. High level officials and department heads are key actors in the politics of application adoption, as each seeks to allocate computing resources differentially in accordance with their perceptions of political advantage or "need." The greater the level of their support for computing, the more likely their efforts to influence computing resource allocation.

The political nature of applications adoption has policy implications for local and federal officials. From the federal standpoint, it suggests that "general" financial support for local government computing might increase capacity, but that capacity will tend to be used primarily for current local priorities. It also suggests that the promulgation of particular computer applications by federal agencies requires that financial support be "earmarked" for those applications. However, unless the application clearly meets locally perceived needs and priorities, some additional carrot or stick incentives might be required to get local agencies to adopt federal perceptions of need or priority. One such carrot is the combination of "general" and "earmarked" support mentioned earlier.

From the local standpoint, it is important to recognize that substantial and continuous infusion of federal financial support can change the existing pattern of applications development in the government. Federal financial support clearly supplements rather than displaces local investment; but the heavy promotion of new development in one area tends to slow down or to retard development in other areas. This occurs because local government computing capacity is fixed at any one time, and can be changed only in large increments over a considerable time period. Most local governments assume that federal support is transitory and therefore shift development priorities temporarily rather than increase capacity. When financial support for an area (e.g., law enforcement) continues at a high rate, the applications development tends to displace other planned development. Over time it therefore changes the pattern of local applications.

CONCLUSION

We presently are uncertain about the extent to which our conclusions about federal policy and computer application diffusion might also apply to other public technologies. However, many of the results of other recent studies in local governments(8) are sufficiently similar to suggest that these results may be generalizable to other public technologies, particularly urban management technologies. Our observations about the local adoption of computing applications have a familiarity when measured against previous "federal pushes" for innovations in local personnel, budgeting, planning, and systems analysis.(9)

Clearly, the design component of policy, in the sense that it reflects the continuity of federal support and the scope of the technology package, is an important variant in most federal diffusion efforts. The "fit" between the federal design approach and local organization and practice will be a key determinant of the speed and extent of local adoptions. In contrast, the selection of transfer mechanisms for a particular technology, as our studies and others suggest,(10) may be primarily contingent upon supplier availability, market demand, local capacity and the compatibility of federal local objectives. Our analyses suggest that in the absence of an assessment of such contingencies, ineffective transfer mechanisms are likely to be selected.

Appendix 1
Data Sources

In conducting the six analyses in this study, data were drawn from a variety of sources. Chief among these was the Urban Information Systems (URBIS) Survey. Other data sources included: the County and City Data Book (1972); a survey of major computer mainframe manufacturers; Datapro 70; the Urban and Regional Information Systems Association (URISA); Datamation; and Computer World. The following sections discuss the data employed from each of these sources.

Urban Information Systems (URBIS) Survey

The data on city and county computing capabilities and characteristics were gathered through a survey conducted by the Public Policy Research Organization (PPRO) of the University of California, Irvine. The survey was supported by the National Science Foundation, Research Applied to National Needs Division. This survey, conducted in 1975, was sent to all cities with a population of 50,000 or more and all counties with populations of 100,000 or more. The purpose of the survey was to gather detailed information on every facet of computing in the local governments surveyed.

Three types of questionnaires were distributed to each city and county government: 1) Chief Executive Views on Data Processing; 2) Local Government Data Processing installation; and 3) Local Government Computing Applications. Mayors, city managers, county supervisors, and county administrative officers received the Chief Executive questionnaire; data processing managers in each installation received the Installation and Applications questionnaires.

The Chief Executive questionnaire was designed to determine attitudes towards EDP and to "identify the important political and administrative characteristics of (the) governments" (Hackathorn, 1975: 2). The Installation and Application questionnaires were designed to determine:

1) organizational arrangements of EDP,

137

2) standard operations and policies of the installation,
3) the officials controlling major departmental decisions,
4) the backgrounds of EDP technical management and staff,
5) financing of EDP,
6) current salaries and expenditures,
7) hardware and software characteristics,
8) computer applications, including transfer data.

Response rates for the three component questionnaires were exceptionally good: 80 percent for the Chief Executive questionnaire, 72 percent for the Installation questionnaire, and 71 percent for the Application questionnaire. To supplement the URBIS survey data and to provide data from the larger system, several other sources of data were employed.

County and City Data Book

The Bureau of the Census, in the County and City Data Book, provides statistical information for cities, counties, Standard Metropolitan Statistical Areas (SMSA), urbanized areas and unincorporated areas. These statistics detail a wide variety of descriptive information on these units, and include such areas as:

1) population and land area,
2) education,
3) labor force
4) families and income,
5) Social Security and public assistance,
6) housing,
7) local government finance,
8) government employment.

This information was used for several purposes, among them identifying characteristics of a local government's environment which might be relevant to internal functioning. Also, the data were used to supplement questionnaire information on a local government's fiscal status. Finally, data on SMSAs was used specifically in the analysis of cooperation in urban intergovernmental networks.

Computer Manufacturers

Information on the location of national offices of computer mainframe manufacturers was obtained directly from 18 manufacturers. Counts were made for each city or county of the number of mainframe manufacturer regional and sales offices. The counts were used in several of the analyses as indicators of supplier availability.

Product and Service Offices

Additional information regarding supplier location was gathered from the 1975 edition of Datapro 70, a guide to manufacturers and suppliers of all types of computer related equipment and services. This source contains the locations of approximately 800 companies. Counts were taken only for companies within each local jurisdiction which were in existence prior to 1971.

The major types of distinctions were drawn between companies in the Datapro 70 survey: product suppliers and service suppliers. The product supplier category included all manufacturers producing physical products for use in computer installations. Some examples of these physical products are: CRT's, Modems and Disks. Specifically excluded from this category were companies that produced such articles as furniture for computer rooms, tape racks, and card trays. The service supplier category consisted of companies which provided two types of services, hardware maintenance and software development (including consulting). When a company was clearly involved in supplying both products and services, it was included in both categories.

Urban and Regional Information Systems Association

The Urban and Regional Information Systems Association (URISA) is an international organization for the advancement of information systems capabilities in urban areas. Membership in URISA brings exposure to other members through the activities of the association, and establishes communication channels through which opportunities for information exchange can arise. New developments in the field of information systems with applications to urban and regional governmental units are introduced to local government through URISA.

Two indicators were used in our analyses to reflect the linkages between urban areas and this professional association. The first was the 1977 distribution by state of URISA members; the second was the average number of annual URISA conference attendees from each state at the 1974-76 URISA conferences.

Article Counts from Datamation, URISA Proceedings, and Computer World

Data on the amount of professional communication regarding specific software applications were obtained through a count of articles published on each type of application in three different computer publications, Datamation, the URISA Proceedings and Computer World. The publication periods which the counts covered were: Datamation, 1958-1974; URISA Proceedings, 1964-1974; and Computer World, 1967-1974.

Appendix 2
Operational Definitions of
the Variables Employed
in the Analyses

CHAPTER 1

Task Complexity*

1 = Recordkeeping – activities which primarily involve the entry, updating, and storage of data.

2 = Calculating/printing – activities which primarily involve sorting, calculating, and printing of stored data to produce specific operational outputs.

3 = Record-restructuring – activities which involve reorganization, reaggregation, and/or analysis of data.

4 = Sophisticated analytics – activities which utilize sophisticated visual, mathematical, simulation or other analytical methods to examine data.

5 = Process control – activities which approximate a cybernetic system; data about the state of a system is continually monitored and fed back to a human or automatic controller which steers the system toward a performance standard.

Pervasiveness

1 = Single function
2 = Multi-function
3 = Organization-wide

---

*Kraemer, Dutton and Matthews (1975).

Communicability

1 = The documentation for less than 75 percent of the applications in use is not adequate for transfer.
2 = The documentation for 75 percent or more of the applications in use is adequate for transfer.

Departure from Current Technologies

100 percent minus the percentage of applications in the same task complexity category previously introduced into the local government system.

Specificity of Evaluation*

1 = Personal evaluation only
2 = Partial measurement (of some aspects of outputs)
3 = Measurements used over virtually the whole output(s), to compare against specification (blueprint or equivalent).

Cost Relative to Other Agency Contributions

Cost to implement relative to all other applications within a particular department.

1 = Low
2 = Medium
3 = High

CHAPTER 2

Need

Revenue-Expenditure Effort
   Mean per capita general revenue – mean per capita general revenue of cities and counties within SMSA. (Source: Census data)

   Mean per capita general expenditure – mean per capita general expenditure of cities and counties within SMSA. (Source: URBIS survey)

Perceived Need
   Chief executive response to survey items on need for cooperation.

---

*Hickson, Pugh and Pheysey (1969).

(Source: URBIS survey)

Supplier Availability
Mainframe Sales Offices – The number of computer mainframe manufacturers' sales offices and regional sales headquarters located within the SMSA. (Sources: Survey of Manufacturers and Datapro)

Product Supplier Sales Offices – The number of computer-related products sales offices located within the SMSA. (Source: Datapro)

Service Suppliers Sales Offices – The number of computer-related services sales offices, such as maintenance and consulting firms, located within the SMSA. (Source: Datapro)

Opportunities

Professionalism
Professional Management Orientation – Degree of use of written objectives and performance measures of programs and services by governmental units within SMSA. (Source: URBIS survey)

Environmental Support
URISA Members – 1976 distribution of Urban and Regional Information Systems Association (URISA) members by state. (Source: URISA)

URISA Conference Participation – Mean number of URISA conference attendees by state, averaged across Montreal, Seattle, and Atlanta conference attendance. (Source: URISA)

Mean Participation – Measure of the degree to which political parties are involved in local politics in the SMSA governmental units. (Source: URBIS survey)

Integration
Degree of Integration – Extent to which data, data processing procedures, and data flow are, or can be linked among computer applications. Mean value for governmental units in SMSA. (Source: URBIS survey)

Supplier Programming
Commercial Programming Mean – Mean across governmental units in SMSA of measure of degree to which commercial software vendors are employed to program computer applications. (Source: URBIS survey)

Hardware Programming Mean – Mean across governmental units in SMSA of measure of degree to which hardware vendors are employed to program computer applications. (Source: URBIS survey)

Cost

Dominance-Equivalence
Difference between the highest and lowest intergovernmental revenue distributed to units within SMSA. (Source: U.S. Census)

Standard deviation of the distribution of the percent of SMSA population contained in each governmental unit within an SMSA. (Source: U.S. Census)

Economic-Wealth Differentials
Difference between the highest and lowest median school years completed by residents of governmental units within SMSA. (Source: U.S. Census)

Difference between the highest and lowest percent unemployed among governmental units within SMSA. (Source: U.S. Census)

Social Status Differentials
Difference between highest and lowest mean vlaue for relative occupational income and educational status of community residents in governmental units within SMSA. (Source: U.S. Census)

Difference between highest and lowest value for a measure of the presence of residents who are likely to require welfare and related poverty-linked services for governmental units within an SMSA. (Source: U.S. Census)

Trade-Off Inducements
Mean amount of funding that was received by governmental units within an SMSA from the following sources: 1) State government; 2) HUD 701; 3) LEAA; 4) Revenue sharing. (Source: URBIS survey)

Slack Resources
Sum of Standardized scores of the following two variables:
1. The difference between authorized and actual data processing personnel for governmental units within an SMSA. (Source: URBIS survey)
2. Total amount of core space available to governmental units; determined by summing core capacity of all data processing installations within a particular unit. (Source: URBIS survey)

Dependent Variables

Diffusion
The four computer applications selected were: revenue forecasting, budget preparation, police service data, and real property records. After selecting the applications, two additional steps were taken to operationalize the diffusion variable. The number of years a particular

application took to diffuse to 50 percent of the adopting population was first calculated. The rate of diffusion to 50 percent of the governmental units within the SMSA was subtracted from the population diffusion rate to provide the score for the dependent variable. Thus, the dependent variable is stated as a positive or negative deviation from the median diffusion rate for the application's diffusion to the entire local government population.

Transfer

The transfer variable was operationalized using questionnaire responses of data processing personnel about the number of applications transferred to a city or county and the sources of these applications. The number of intra-SMSA transfers were aggregated and this number was divided by the number of general governments within the SMSA included in the sample.

Resource Sharing

To measure the resource sharing variable, an index was created to reflect the extent to which each city or county in the SMSA used cooperative organizational arrangements in the delivery of data processing services. A score of one was assigned if data processing was an autonomous activity of the local government, a score of two if it was provided by some combination of independent and cooperative organizational arrangements, and a score of three if it was provided entirely through cooperative arrangements. A mean score for each SMSA was computed from this index.

CHAPTER 4

Frequency of Data Generation; Frequency of Use of the Output

1 = very infrequently (e.g., quarterly or semi-annually)
2 = infrequently (e.g., monthly)
3 = uncertain/neither frequently nor infrequently
4 = frequently (e.g., daily)
5 = very frequently (e.g., continuously)

Transitivity

1 = task accomplishment: a resource used primarily in the accomplishment of organizational tasks
2 = mixed: a resource use for both organizational task accomplishment and organizational maintenance
3 = maintenance: a resource used primarily for organizational maintenance

Pervasiveness

1 = single function
2 = multi-function
3 = organization-wide

Professional Communication

Sum of the standard scores for the number of published articles on an application in three professional publications, the URISA Proceedings, Datamation, and Computer World.

Relative Earliness of an Application's First Adoption

100 percent minus the percentage of applications in the same task complexity category previously introduced into the local government system. The five categories were:*

1. Recordkeeping – activities which primarily involve the entry, updating, and storage of data.
2. Calculating/printing – activities which primarily involve sorting, calculating, and printing of stored data to produce specific operational outputs.
3. Record-restructuring – activities which involve reorganization, reaggregation, and/or analysis of data.
4. Sophisticated analytics – activities which utilize sophisticated visual, mathematical, simulation or other analytical methods to examine data.
5. Process control – activities which approximate a cybernetic system; data about the state of a system is continually monitored and fed back to a human or automatic controller which steers the system towards a performance standard.

URISA Membership

1976 distribution of Urban Regional Information Systems Association (URISA) members by state.

URISA Conference Attendance

Number of URISA conference attendees by state, averaged across 1974, 1975, and 1976 conference attendance.

---

*Adapted from Kraemer, et al. (1976) and Danziger (1977).

Computer Manufacturer Mainframe Sales Offices

The number of computer mainframe manufacturers' sales offices and regional sales headquarters located within the city or county.

Computer Service Supplier Sales Offices

The number of computer-related services sales offices, such as maintenance and consulting firms, located within city or county.

Staff Experience

Sum of 6 questionnaire items:

% analysts 0-2 years experience x 1
% analysts 3-5 years experience x 4
% analysts over 5 years experience x 5
% programmers 0-2 years experience x 1
% programmers 3-5 years experience x 4
% programmers over 5 years experience x 5

Staff Skill Level
Sum of number of analysts and programmers with skills in:

A. Teleprocessing
B. Simulations
C. Statistical analysis
D. Data base management systems
E. Geographic data
F. Graphics

Agency Effectiveness in Using Computing

Three-point scale based upon chief executive responses to questionnaire items on which units use the computer most effectively and least effectively:

1 = agency mentioned by chief executive as using computing least effectively.
2 = agency mentioned as neither an effective nor ineffective user of computing.
3 = agency mentioned by chief executive as using computing most effectively.

Need

Standardized score for each application of the standardized indicators below:

1. Periodical holdings – Total population, 1970
2. Data dictionary – (Total number of operational applications + degree of integration among computer applications) /2.
3. Federal and state grant files – (% intergovernmental revenue of total revenue + amount of intergovernmental revenue) /2.
4. Alias name file and wants/warrants file – (Total serious crimes + crime rate) /2.
5. Cash management/cash flow analysis – (Bond rating from Moody's manual + total general revenue (in millions)) /2.
6. Employee records – Total full time equivalent local government employees.
7. Budgeting – Program structure related to line-item budget – (Total general expenditure + per capita expenditure) /2.
8. Payroll preparation/accounting – Employee payroll (in millions).
9. Real property records – (Land area in square miles + % owner occupancy + % property tax of total revenue) /3.

Specificity of Evaluation*

1 = personal evaluation only
2 = partial measurement (of some aspects of outputs)
3 = measurements used over virtually the whole output(s), to compare against specification (blueprint or equivalent)

Cost Relative to Other Agency Applications

Cost to implement relative to all other applications within a particular department.

1 = low
2 = medium
3 = high

---

*See Hickson, et al. (1969: 383).

Agency Budget

Total expenditures (in dollars) of the governmental agency using the application (1972 Census of Governments)

Agency Expenditure as a Percentage of Total Governmental unit expenditure

Agency expenditures/total governmental unit expenditure (1972 Census of Governments)

External Funding of EDP

Sum of responses of data processing managers to the following question-naire items: "Approximately how much was received in the last fiscal year from this source?" – 1) State; 2) HUD 701 funds; 3) LEAA funds; 4) Federal revenue sharing.

External Funding of EDP as a Percentage of Total EDP Budget

External funding of EDP/Total EDP budget, 1973

CHAPTER 5

Development Status

An index of the level of information processing development constructed by Guttman scaling of five different information processing tasks: recordkeeping, calculating/printing, record restructuring, sophisticated analytics, and process control. These information processing tasks are theoreticallyindicative of a progression from minor to major restructuring of the information flows within the organization. Cut points for the scale were based on the following criteria:

1 = local governments with no more than one application in any of the categories
two or more applications in the calculating/printing, or calculating-printing and recordkeeping categories
3 = two or more applications in the preceding two categories as well as record restructuring and sophisticated analytics
4 = two or more applications in each of the five information processing categories

The coefficient of reproducibility for the development status scale is .93.

Climate Favorableness

Sum of scores from two Likert-scaled items indicating the chief executive's perception of the favorableness of (a) the local legislative body and (b) department heads towards the expansion of data processing. Coefficient alpha for this index is .64.

Climate Heterogeneity

This index is measured by scaling the two items in the climate favorableness index according to how the chief executive perceived the attitudes of the local legislative body and department heads as differing from one another regarding the expansion of data processing in the government.

1 = complete lack of agreement, e.g., chief executive perceives legislative body as strongly opposed to the expansion of data processing, but department heads strongly favorable to its expansion.

2 = moderate disagreement, e.g., chief executive perceives legislative body as moderately opposed or indifferent to the expansion of data processing, but department heads moderately favorable to its expansion.

3 = slight disagreement, e.g., chief executive perceives legislative body as moderately favorable to the expansion of data processing, but department heads strongly favorable to its expansion.

4 = complete agreement.

Chief Executive Support

This index taps the difference between the executive's perception of the expected utility of computing innovation and the executive's perception of the current utility of the technology. The more positive the difference between the executive's perception of expected and current utility, the greater his support; the more negative the difference, the less his support. The current and expected utility scales were derived from chief executive responses to the following items:

Current Utility

Item
1. In general, computers provide information which is helpful to me in making decisions.
2. The computer makes information available to department heads that was not available before.
3. The computer is an essential tool in the day-to-day operations of this government.
4. Computing and data processing have generally failed to live up to my original expectations. (Reversed)
5. For the most part, computers have clearly increased the speed and

ease of performance of government operations where they have been applied.

6. The use of computers and data processing results in greater cooperation among the operating departments and agencies.
7. I have indicated to department heads that computers and data processing should be used wherever economically feasible in this government.

Expected Utility

1. In the future, the computer will become much more essential in the day-to-day operations of this government.
2. In the future, a large proportion of this local government's budget should support computers and data processing.
3. If properly designed and managed, much of the data gathered by this government in its daily operations could be collected and organized in ways that provide useful information about community conditions and government operations.

Factor analysis of the ten items resulted in two independent factors with average loadings of .56 for the current utility items and .50 for the expected utility items. The average inter-item correlations for the current and expected utility items were .34 and .28 respectively. In constructing the scales, the raw scores for the items were summed and the scales were then converted to standard scores. Coefficient alpha for the current utility scale is .80 and for the expected utility scale is .67.

Professionalism

Professionalism measures several operating policies which reflect the use of professional practices within the legislative and administrative components of the local government. Included in the index are scores for council member's annual salary, presence or absence of councilmember staff, number of services provided councilmembers, and the use by the organization of written program objectives and measures of performance.

Resource Allocation

The natural log of the local government's data processing budget.

Slack Resources

Measured by adding the standard scores for two indicators. The first indicator was a measure of personnel slack represented by the number of actual data processing personnel as a percentage of authorized personnel. The second indicator was a measure of machine slack operationalized by the amount of core space available in the city.

User Involvement

User involvement was operationalized by summing the standard scores for indices of user participation in four computer application activities: adoption, design, development, and evaluation. Data processing installation directors in each local government responded to 13 questions which were used to create the index. The items are as follows:

1. User department has major input to adoption of new applications.
2. User department has authority for setting priorities for development of new applications.
3. Users participate in assigning priorities to projects.
4. Users initiate major changes of EDP applications.
5. User department designs applications.
6. Users work as member of technical group.
7. Users review designs.
8. User department programs applications.
9. Users provide test data.
10. Users sign off accepting applications.
11. Users study anticipated benefits and costs.
12. Users study actual benefits and costs.
13. Users formally evaluate applications they use.

Innovation Scope and Magnitude

The number of computer applications in development was used to measure innovation adoption. Since many of the organizations in the survey had automated some information processing tasks, corrections had to be made in the outcome variables to account for existing applications. Innovation magnitude was operationalized by dividing the total number of computer applications in development by the total number of non-automated tasks. Because 260 applications were identified in the survey of computer software, the number of non-automated tasks was measured by subtracting the number of applications already operational from 260. The scope of innovation was measured by dividing the number of functional units which had not previously automated any tasks. Thirty-two functional units were defined for local government organizations (e.g., police, fire, libraries). Thus, the number of possible functional areas was 32 minus the functional areas with operational applications.

Notes

INTRODUCTION

(1) Consequently, this book is addressed to national concerns such as those expressed in the report of the Office of National R&D Assessment (1975).

(2) The concept of revenue maintenance is suggested by Aaron Wildavsky who describes such behavior as emphasizing control through the generation of a revenue surplus and the limitation of expenditures. See Wildavsky (1975).

(3) Colton indicates that LEAA funding, particularly that beginning with the Safe Streets and Crime Control Act, has had substantial impact on police and other local law enforcement computing. See Colton (1978).

(4) The Department of Health, Education and Welfare and the Department of Labor have provided the largest proportion of financial assistance to state and local governments (about 60 percent of the total annual aid). However, it is possible that since this aid frequently goes through the states, relatively little has reached local governments for automation in the human resources area. Federal assistance for community development and public works, mainly from the Departments of Housing and Urban Development and Transportation, has been less than 10 percent of the total annual aid and has come and gone with various federal urban programs. This is based on unpublished data produced in response to Office of Management and Budget Bulletin No. 72-1 (OMB, 1971).

(5) This duality of objectives is illustrated by the following rationale for the USAC Program:

> There are many reasons that the Federal Government might wish to develop urban information systems for governments below their own level. For one, the Federal Government finds itself pulled more and more into local problems with such programs as Model Cities, to cite

one example . . . Moreover, the Federal Government has depended upon municipal government for much of the information which it used in attempting to provide national services. Unless the information fed from the local level can be improved, many of the services provided by the Federal Government will be inefficient at best, and quite often totally useless. (Government Data Systems, 1971, pp. 6-7).

USAC stands for Urban Information Systems Inter-Agency Committee. The primary goal of the USAC Program was the creation of prototype integrated municipal information systems in six municipalities. Overall, $26 million was spent on the USAC Program over the five-year span of its research and development. Of this, the federal agencies contributed $20 million, and the six municipalities the remainder. See Government Data Systems (1971) and Nation's Cities (1972).

CHAPTER 1

(1) The definition of diffusion has remained relatively stable over the period the concept has garnered the attention of social scientists. Rogers and Shoemaker define the concept as "the process by which innovations spread to members of a social system." In a recent study of diffusion of innovations in municipal governments, Feller and Menzel employ a more detailed definition: "the rate and extent of acceptance and use of innovations among a class of adopters and the process(es) by which individual adopters interact with one another and with other change agents." See Rogers and Shoemaker (1971: 12) and Feller and Menzel (1976: 2).

(2) Diffusion researchers have amassed a large body of literature with probably over 2,500 sources to date. Review of such a massive body of literature is obviously beyond the scope here. We therefore focus on three recent critiques.

(3) See, for example, Robert W. Backoff (1974) and Dean Schooler, Jr. (1970).

(4) With the exception of Mansfield's research on innovation by the firm, the studies cited by Rogers and Shoemaker in relation to propositions on innovation attributes are almost universally grounded in rural sociology. See Rogers and Shoemaker (1971: 350-352).

(5) There is seeming disagreement in the literature about the amount of research on innovation attributes. Warner (1974) and Downs and Mohr (1975) note that few empirical studies have been conducted on innovation attributes. Rogers and Shoemaker (1971), on the other hand, provide over 50 citations to studies of innovation attributes. This disagreement is partly attributable to differences in the definition of innovation attributes. Rogers and Shoemaker use "perceived attributes" as the operative definition. Downs and Mohr refer to "invariant characteristics" (therefore characteristics not subject to perceptual differences), suggesting a distinction between their definition and that of Rogers and Shoemaker.

(6) Although Feller and Menzel (1976) employ curve fitting, they also cite the noteworthy criticisms of L. Nabseth and G.F. Ray (1974). A more recent criticism with suggestions for an alternative approach is provided by Eyestone (1977).

(7) The problem of primary attribute variation and instability in diffusion research findings is discussed in Downs and Mohr (1975).

(8) Our use of the term policy coincides with its use in James F. Reynolds (1975).

(9) In a study of farm practices, Fleigel and Kivlin (1966) used the average percentage of adoptions per year for the eight consecutive years of most rapid adoption of measure rate of adoption. The differences in the "constants" associated with each measure (i.e., a specified percentage of the population for the Rogers and Shoemaker (1971) measure and a specified number of years of most rapid adoption for the Fleigel and Kivlin measure) suggest that the rate of diffusion for a given innovation might vary significantly between the measures.

(10) Our earlier criticism of the assumptions of curve fitting as a methodology for analyzing innovation diffusion is the basis for the creation of the third dependent variable. We noted that curve fitting is not an adequate test of theoretical relevance and that it generally ignores constant source diffusion.   Furthermore, since curve fitting requires an estimate of the maximum proportion of adopters, it also fails to explain why a particular innovation diffuses to only X percent of the population. Recognizing that the extent and rate of diffusion and the time of introduction of an innovation differ among innovations, it would be useful to employ a number of these dimensions simultaneously as an outcome variable. Such an approach requires few assumptions than curve fitting, accounts for more dimensions of variation in diffusion patterns, and does not rely on making inferences about diffusion processes directly from diffusion curves.

In a recent critique of research on the diffusion of policy innovations among the states, Eyestone (1977) suggests a methodology similar to that set forth here. He argues: "We do not yet know enough about policy content . . . to risk the confusions of lumping together large numbers of policies especially if in doing so we would be mixing representatives of several distinct diffusion models . . . Comparison of diffusion patterns may provide a way of generating policy clusters empirically according to their political similarity." Although Eyestone's suggestion points in the right direction, it requires considerable faith that the representations of distinct diffusion models will not be confused because of variance in diffusion factors unrelated to policy content. The approach we use here reflects the view that the effects of neither primary nor secondary attributes should be subject to a priori assumption.

(11) Rogers and Shoemaker (1971: 154) define complexity as the "degree to which an innovation is perceived as relatively difficult to understand and use." Lin and Zaltman (1973: 103) refine this definition by suggesting that

"complexity may become manifest on two levels: 1) The innovation may contain a complex idea; 2) The implementation of the innovation may be complex." Our definition of task complexity refers to the latter of these two types of complexity.

(12) See Haberstroh (1965) and Wynne and Dickson (1975).

(13) See Downs and Mohr (1975) for a discussion of some of the sources of instability in innovation diffusion research findings.

(14) Wilks' lambda, a measure of the discriminating power of the variables, was .40 before any discriminant functions were removed. This indicates considerable discriminating power among the innovation attributes and policy variables.

(15) Several of the variables contribute very little to the discriminating power of any of the discriminant functions. Among the innovation attributes, task complexity and relative agency cost add little discriminating power. The magnitudes of the locus of development and professional communication coefficients in each of the two functions are also relatively small. Departure from existing technologies and federal financial assistance are the only two variables significant in each of the two functions.

CHAPTER 2

(1) One application was selected from each of four empirically-derived diffusion categories. The description of the category and the application associated with each are: 1) Moderate diffusion with a brief flurry of adoption near the end of the period – revenue forecasting; 2) Moderate diffusion with adoption beginning early in the period and continuing at a relatively constant level – budget preparation; 3) Extensive diffusion with rapid adoption occurring near the end of the period – police service data; 4) extensive diffusion with first adoptions early in the period and continuing at a high level through most of the period – real property records. For a discussion of the development of these categories, see Chapter 1.

(2) For a summary and critique of some of the assertions about resource utilization and technology transfer, see Chapter 3 and Kraemer (1977).   .

CHAPTER 3

(1) An interesting example of the portability notion can be found in former President Nixon's, March 1972, speech to Congress on Science and Technology:

Federal research and development activities generate a great deal of new technology which can be applied in ways that go well beyond the immediate mission of the supporting agency. In such cases, I believe, the government has a responsibility to transfer the results of its research and development activities to wider use in the private sector.

(2) The questions primarily used in this analysis asked about transfers from another local government (city, county, school district, special district or regional agency). The survey did not specifically request information about transfers from federal or state agencies, computer manufacturers, software vendors, or organizations which specialize in urban technology transfer (e.g., Public Technology, Inc.). These data were collected indirectly through a checklist of computer applications which included major "transfer packages," particularly those available from federal agencies. In addition, some of the respondents listed computer applications from these non-local government sources in their replies about transfers from other local governments. These non-local sources are included in the data presented here and treated separately wherever possible. However, since the survey did not specifically ask about these non-local government sources, the data about these sources should be considered only suggestive.

(3) The experiences of the authors in extensive field studies in U.S. cities verify this fact graphically. One of the most common complaints heard in city data processing establishments with considerable transfer experience was that the costs of answering inquiries related to transfer were exceeding any benefit the city might receive. In most of these cases, the city management was preparing to either cease answering transfer inquiries or to begin charging for service.

(4) A good example of an organization that allows only larger, more sophisticated users is MIX (Metropolitan Information Exchange), an organization of local government IBM computer users. Membership in MIX is limited to those cities and counties with very large IBM computers. These are typically the larger, more sophisticated data processing installations.

(5) This is suggested indirectly by the finding (Table 17) that 72 percent of the transfers take place among sites with the same brand of computer mainframe.

(6) Data base management systems are a good example of an advanced technology that enriches the designer's job (and perhaps the system's utility to users as well) but reduces the possibility of widespread transfer of applications developed on them. For example, Donald Luria, the former technical director of the Charlotte, North Carolina USAC project, points out the following barriers to application transfer from these systems:

Computer programs that run under a particular data management system rarely, if ever, can be transferred to run under another data management system.

. . . The structure of an integrated data base is a more subtle barrier to program transfer. In a job or application-oriented (non-integrated) system the files are structured to meet the processing requirements of a single or relatively small number of programs. In an integrated data base the files should be structured to optimize the service to a multitude of users. It follows then that computer programs that work efficiently against one file structure may be far from efficient against another file structure. Since the structure is a function of the nature and variety of applications and these will vary from city-to-city, another barrier to the transfer of programs is set in place. (Luria, 1973, p. 290).

Yet, even without frills, user-oriented design reduces the likelihood of transfer. For example, Luria also says:

. . . there is an inverse relationship between the degree to which the system is operations based and integrated and the degree to which the systems programs are transferable. First, the more operationally based a system is, the more the programs become tailored to specific user-oriented procedures. (Luria, 1973, p. 286).

(7) In some cases, and particularly in development projects supported by the federal government, there is added money offered to make the development generalized for transferability. Even so, in these cases one can find examples of technical people working to meet local needs at the expense of general problems. Two authors, Fossum and Gottlieb, question whether the result of design for transfer is worth the price either for the development city or another transfer city. See Fossum and Gottlieb (1973).

CHAPTER 4

(1) The concept of "information processing task" is an analytic taxonomy which is based on the primary modality of an automated application. It is discussed in Kraemer, et al. (1976) and Danziger (1977).

(2) The ten computer applications selected, representative of six different diffusion patterns, were: 1) library periodical holdings; 2) data processing data dictionary; 3) federal and state grant file(s); 4) alias name file; 5) cash management/cash flow analysis; 6) wants/warrants file; 7) employee records; 8) program structure related to line-item budget; 9) payroll preparation/accounting; 10) real property records. For a discussion of the development of the diffusion categories and their description, see Chapter 1.

(3) See Fliegel and Kivlin (1966), p. 244. Our definition of risk differs from the classical economic use of risk in that it does not incorporate decision maker utilities or preferences. Rather, as it is used here, risk focuses on factors likely to influence decision maker certainty and concern about cause-effect relationships associated with the innovation's costs and benefits. For a discussion of risk and innovation in state and local government, see Feller (1977).

(4) Such data transformations are discussed in Kruskal (1972), pp. 182-192.

CHAPTER 5

(1) Rogers and Agarwala-Rogers (1976) indicate that slack resources has seldom been operationalized with much precision and that it should be operationalized as a multi-dimensional variable. Although the measure used here falls short of an ideal one, we have attempted to take their suggestions into account.

(2) A notion allied with that of slack resources is slack innovation. Mohr (1969: 126) writes that "after solution of immediate problems, the quest for organizational effectiveness or corporate profit motivates the adoption of most new programs and technologies." Since prestige is often defined as a resource in the organizational literature, this third concept might be viewed as concerned with creating resources relevant to future allocation decisions (Thompson, 1967: 33-34). Unlike resource allocation and slack resources, which are distinguishable from the other concepts already discussed, slack innovation is highly related to the state of development of technology within an organization. We therefore do not conceive of it independently from the developmental status of the technology.

(3) The conceptualization and measurement of one of the variables, chief executive support, is discussed at greater length in the following chapter.

CHAPTER 6

(1) Factor analysis of the ten items resulted in two independent factors with average loadings of .56 for the current utility items and .50 for the expected utility items. The average inter-item correlations for the current and expected utility items were .34 and .28, respectively. In constructing the scales, the raw scores for the items were summed and the scales were then converted to standard scores. Coefficient alpha for the current utility scale is .80 and for the expected utility scale is .67.

CHAPTER 7

(1) All other comprehensive financial systems such as ARMS (Accounting and Resources Management System), and IFMS (Integrated Financial Management System) also were predicted as not likely to be widely adopted by local governments.

(2) Nan Lin and Gerald Zaltman, "Dimensions and innovations," in Processes and Phenomena of Social Change, ed. Gerald Zaltman (New York: Wiley, 1973), pp. 93-116 at 109.

(3) See Chapter 4 and Kenneth L. Kraemer, "Local government, information

systems, and technology transfer," Public Administration Review, Vol. 7, No. 4 (July/August 1977).

(4) Everett M. Rogers, "Effects of incentives on the diffusion of innovations: The case of family planning in Asia," in Processes and Phenomena of Social Change, ed. Gerald Zaltman (New York: Wiley, 1973), pp. 133-152.

(5) The shortcomings and limited utility of federal demonstration projects do not appear to be limited to computing. See Walter S. Baer, Leland L. Johnson and Edward W. Merrow, An Analysis of Federally Funded Demonstration Projects: Final Report (Santa Monica, CA: Rand, 1976).

(6) Rogers, et al., The Innovation Process in Public Organizations: Some Elements of a Preliminary Model, 1977.

(7) George F. Break, Intergovernmental Fiscal Relations in the United States (Washington, D.C.: Brookings, 1967).

(8) See, for example, the recent studies of Richard D. Bingham, The Adoption of Innovation by Local Government (Milwaukee, WI: Marquette University, Office of Urban Research, 1975); Irwin Feller and Donald Menzel, Diffusion of Innovations in Municipal Governments (University Park, PA: Institute for Research on Human Resources, 1976); and Robert K. Yin, Karen A. Heald, Mary E. Vogel, Patricia D. Fleischauer and Bruce C. Vladek, A Review of Case Studies in Technological Innovations in State and Local Services (Washington, D.C.: The Rand Corporation, 1976).

(9) Ida A. Hoos, Systems Analysis in Public Policy (Berkeley, CA: University of California Press, 1972); and Allen Schick, Budget Innovation in the States (Washington, D.C.: Brookings Institution, 1971).

(10) Yin, et al., A Review of Case Studies on Technological Innovations in State and Local Services; Feller and Menzel, "Diffusion of Innovations in Municipal Governments;" House et al., Making Federal R&D Useful: A Case Study of the Implementation Process; Rogers, et al., The Innovation Process in Public Organization: Some Elements of a Preliminary Model; Henry W. Lambright and Albert Teich, Federal Laboratories and Technology Transfer: Institutions, Linkages and Processes (Syracuse, N.Y.: Syracuse University Research Corporation, 1974).

References

Ackoff, R. Redesigning the Future: A Systems Approach to Societal Problems. New York: Wiley, 1974.

Aiken, M., and J. Hage. "Organizational interdependence and intraorganizational structure." American Sociological Review 23 (1968 December): 912-930.

Arthur D. Little, Inc., and Industrial Research Institute. Barriers to Innovation in Industry: Opportunities for Public Policy Changes. Washington, D.C.: Arthur D. Little, 1973.

Backoff, R.W. "Operationalizing administrative reform for improved governmental performance." Administration and Society 6 (1974 May): 73-106.

Baer, W.S., L.L. Johnson, and E.W. Merrow. An Analysis of Federally Funded Demonstration Projects: Final Report. Santa Monica, CA: Rand, 1976.

Bingham, R.D. The Adoption of Innovation by Local Government. Milwaukee, WI: Marquette University, Office of Urban Research, 1975a.

_____. "Innovation in local government: The case of public housing." Paper presented at the Midwest Political Science Association Annual Meeting, Chicago, 1975b.

Break, G.F. Intergovernmental Fiscal Relations in the United States. Washington, D.C.: Brookings, 1967.

Colton, K.W. Police and Computer Technology: Use, Implementation and Impact. Lexington, MA: Lexington Books, 1978.

Crawford, R. "The application of science and technology in local government in the United States." Studies in Comparative Local Government 7 (1973) (2): 1-19.

Crecine, J.P. "A computer simulation model of municipal budgeting." Management Science 13 (1967 July): 786-815.

_____. Governmental Problem Solving: A Computer Simulation of Municipal Budgeting. Chicago: Rand-McNally, 1969.

Cyert, R.M., and J.G. March. A Behavioral Theory of the Firm. Englewood Cliffs, N.J.: Prentice-Hall, 1963.

Danziger, J.N. "Computers, local governments, and the litany to EDP." Public Administration Review 37 (1977 January/February): 28-37.

Danziger, J.N., and W.H. Dutton. "Technological innovation in local government: The case of computing." Policy and Politics 6 (1977 September): 127-49.

Davis, R.M. "Federal interest in computer utilization by state and local governments." The Bureaucrat 1 (1972) (4): 349-356.

Dennis, J. "Support for the institution of elections by the mass public." American Political Science Review 64 (1970 September).

Downs, A. "A realistic look at the final payoffs from urban data systems." Public Administration Review 27 (1967, May/June): 204-210.

Downs, G.W. Jr. Bureaucracy, Innovation and Public Policy. Lexington, MA: Lexington Books, 1976.

Downs, G.W. Jr., and L.B. Mohr. "Conceptual issues in the study of innovation." Paper prepared for delivery at the 1975 Annual Meeting of the American Political Science Association, San Francisco, 1975.

_____. "Conceptual issues in the study of innovation." Administrative Science Quarterly 21 (1976 December): 700-714.

Dror, Y. "Administrative agencies and courts: Some patterns of interorganizational relations." International Review of Administrative Sciences 30 (1964): 285-286.

Dutton, W.H., and K.L. Kraemer. "Determinants of support for computerized information systems." Midwest Review of Public Administration, March 1978.

Easton, D. A Systems Analysis of Political Life. New York: Wiley, 1965.

Eyestone, R. "Confusion, diffusion and innovation." American Political Science Review 71 (1977 June): 441-447.

Federal Council on Science and Technology. Directory of Federal Technology Transfer. Washington, D.C.: Government Printing Office, 1975.

Feller, I. "Uncertainty and risk in the adoption of technological innovations by state and municipal governments." University Park, PA: Institute for Research on Human Resources, 1977. Mimeographed.

Feller, I., and D.C. Menzel. "Diffusion milieux as a focus of research on innovation in the public sector." Paper presented at the Annual Meeting of the American Political Science Association, San Francisco, 1975.

_____. Diffusion of Innovations in Municipal Governments. University Park, PA: Institute for Research on Human Resources, 1976.

Feller, I., D.C. Menzel, & A.J. Engel. Diffusion of Technology in State Mission-Oriented Agencies. University Park, PA: The Pensylvania State University, Center for the Study of Science Policy, 1974.

Fliegel, F., and J. Kivlin. "Attributes of innovations as factors in diffusion." American Journal of Sociology 31 (1966 November): 235-248.

Fossum, B., and S. Gottlieb. "The Wichita Falls USAC project viewed in perspective," pp. 380-385 in Urban and Regional Information Systems: Information Research for an Urban Society, Vol. I, Papers from the Tenth Annual Conference of URISA. Claremont, CA: URISA, 1973.

Friesma, P.H. "Interjurisdictional agreements in metropolitan areas." Administrative Science Quarterly 15 (1970 June): 242-252.

Government Data Systems. "USAC: Federal funding for municipal information systems." Government Data Systems 1 (1971 July/August): 6-24.

Gray, V. "Innovation in the states: A diffusion study." American Political Science Review 67 (1973 December): 1174-1185.

Haberstroh, C. "Organization design and system analysis," in Handbook of Organizations. Chicago: Rand-McNally, 1965.

Hackathorn, L.D. The URBIS Census Survey: A Description and Evaluation of Data Collection Procedures and Response Patterns. Irvine, CA: Public Policy Research Organization, University of California, Irvine, 1975.

Hage, J. and M. Aiken. "Program change and organizational properties: A comparative analysis." American Journal of Sociology 72 (1967 March): 503-518.

Havelock, R. Planning for Innovation through Dissemination and Utilization of Knowledge. Ann Arbor, MI: The University of Michigan, 1969.

Hayes, F.O.R. "Innovation in state and local government," pp. 1-23 in F.O.R. Hayes and J. Rasmussen (eds.) Centers for Innovation in Cities and States. San Francisco: San Francisco Press, 1972.

Hemmens, G.C. "Implementing the integrated municipal information systems concept: The Charlotte, North Carolina Case." Paper presented at the 57th Annual Conference of the American Institute of Planners, San Antonio, Texas, 1975.

Hershman, A. "A mess in MIS." Dun's Review (1968 January): 26-27 and 85-87.

Hickson, D.H.; D.S. Pugh; and D.C. Pheysey. "Operations technology and organization structure: An empirical reappraisal." Administrative Science Quarterly 14 (1969 September): 378-397.

Honnold, J.A., and P.E. Erickson. "Technology and organization: Measurement strategies." Paper presented at the 69th Annual Meeting of the American Sociological Association, Montreal, 1974.

Hoos, I.A. Systems Analysis in Public Policy. Berkeley, CA: University of California Press, 1972.

House, P.W.; D.W. Jones; and O.M. Bevilacqua. Making Federal R&D Useful: A Case Study of the Implementation Process. Berkeley, CA: The Institute of Transportation Studies, 1977.

Illich, I. Tools for Conviviality. New York: Harper and Row, 1973.

International City Management Association. "Managing data for decisions." Public Management 53 (1971 October).

_____. "Innovations in local governments." Public Management 57 (1975 April).

James, L.R., and A.P. Jones. "Organizational climate: A review of theory and research." Psychological Bulletin 18 (1974 December): 1096-1112.

Kelman, H.C., and D.P. Warwick. "Bridging micro and macro approaches to social change: A social-psychological perspective," pp. 13-74 in Gerald Zaltman (ed.) Processes and Phenomena of Social Change. New York: Wiley, 1973.

Kling, R. "Automated information systems in public policymaking." Irvine, CA: Public Policy Research Organization, Working Paper 76-16, 1976.

Kraemer, K.L. "USAC: An evolving intergovernmental mechanism for urban information systems development." Public Administration Review 31 (1971 September/October): 543-551.

_____. "Local government, information systems, and technology transfer: Evaluating some common assertions about transfer of computer applications." Public Administration Review 37 (1977 July/August): 368-382.

Kraemer, K.L.; W.H. Dutton; and J.R. Matthews. "Municipal computers:

Growth, usage and management." Urban Data Service Report 7 (1975a November): 1-15.

Kraemer, K.L.; J.N. Danziger; W.H. Dutton; and S. Pearson. "Chief executives, local governments, and computers." Nation's Cities 13 (1975b October): 17-40.

Kraemer, K.L.; J.N. Danziger; W.H. Dutton; A. Mood; and R.Kling. "A future cities survey research design for policy analysis." Socio-Economic Planning Sciences 10 (1976 September): 199-211.

Kraemer, K.L., and J.L. King. Computers, Power and Urban Management: What Every Local Executive Should Know. Beverly Hills, CA.: Sage, 1967a.

_____. "The URBIS project: A policy-oriented study of computing in local government," pp. 406-429 in Computers, Local Government and Productivity, Vol. I, Papers from the Thirteenth Annual Conference of URISA. Chicago: URISA, 1976b.

Kraemer, K.L.; J.N. Danziger; and J.L. King. "Information technology and urban management in the United States," in Information Technology and Local Government. Paris: Organization for Economic Cooperation and Development, 1978.

Kruskal, J.B. "Statistical analysis: Transformations of data." International Encyclopedia of the Social Sciences, (1972): 182-192.

Lambright, W.H., and A.H. Teich. Federal Laboratories and Technology Transfer: Institutions, Linkages and Processes. Syracuse, N.Y.: Syracuse University Research Corporation, 1974.

_____. "Technology transfer as a problem in interorganizational relationships." Administration and Society 8 (1976 May): 29-54.

Lambright, W.H., and P.J. Flynn. "Bureaucratic politics and technological change in Syracuse and Rochester: Notes on work in progress." Paper presented at the 1976 Annual Meeting of the American Political Science Association, Chicago, 1976.

Levine, S.; P.E. White; and B.D. Paul. "Community interorganizational problems in providing medical care and social services." American Journal of Public Health 53 (1963): 1183-1195.

Lin, N., and G. Zaltman. "Dimensions of innovations," pp. 93-116 in G. Zaltman (ed.) Processes and Phenomena of Social Change. New York: Wiley: 1973.

Lindblom, C.E. "The science of muddling through." Public Administration Review 19 (1959 Fall): 79-88.

Lucas, H.C., Jr. Why Information Systems Fail. New York: Columbia University Press, 1975.

Luria, D.D. "Success depends on transferability," pp. 286-293 in Urban and Regional Information Systems: Information Research for an Urban Society, Vol. I, Papers from the Tenth Annual Conference of URISA. Claremont, CA: URISA, 1973.

Marrett, C. "On the specification of interorganizational dimensions." Sociology and Social Research 56 (1971): 83-97.

Matthews, J.R.; W.H. Dutton; and K.L. Kraemer. "County Computers: Growth, usage and management." Urban Data Service Report 8 (1976 February).

McKinsey & Co. "The 1968 McKinsey report on computer utilization," pp. 94-172 in Management Information Systems. Baltimore: Penguin Books, 1971.

Miller, T. "The utility and timeliness of research on meeting local needs for science and technology." Remarks prepared for delivery at the Annual Meeting of the American Political Science Association, Washington, D.C., September 1-4, 1977.

Miller, W.B. "Inter-institutional conflict as a major impediment to delinquency prevention." Human Organizations 17 (1958): 20-23.

Moch, M. "Structure and organizational resource allocation." Administrative Science Quarterly 21 (1976 December): 661-674.

Mohr, L.B. "Determinants of innovation in organizations." American Political Science Review 63 (1969 March): 111-126.

Nabseth, L., and G.F. Ray. The Diffusion of New Industrial Processes. London: Cambridge University Press, 1974.

National Aeronautics and Space Administration. Spinoff 1976: A Bicentennial Report. Washington, D.C.: NASA, Technology Utilization Office, 1976.

National Commission on Productivity. Policy Statement of September 7, 1971. Washington, D.C.: National Commission on Productivity, 1971.

National Technical Information Service. Directory of Computerized Data Files and Related Software Available from Federal Agencies. Washington, D.C.: U.S. Department of Commerce, 1974.

Nation's Cities. "City hall's approaching revolution in service delivery." Nation's Cities 10 (1972 January): 11-46.

Nelson, R., and S. Winter. "Growth theory from an evolutionary perspective: The differential productivity puzzle." American Economic Review 65 (1975 May): 338-344.

Nolan, D. "The Fresno city experience in transfer or translation of a financial information system using USAC technology," pp. 245-252 in Computers, Local Government and Productivity, Vol. II, Papers presented at the Thirteenth Annual Conference of URISA. Chiago: URISA, 1976.

Office of National R & D Assessment. Official Program Plan for Support of Extramural Research. Washington, D.C.: National Science Foundation, 1975.

OMB. Office of Management and Budget, Bulletin No.72-1.Washington, D.C.: Executive Office of the President, July 9, 1971.

Organization for Economic Cooperation and Development. The Conditions for Success in Technological Innovation. Paris: OECD, 1971.

Paul, J.R., and J.L. McCarty. "FAMIS – A study of system transferability," pp. 99-115 in Urban and Regional Information Systems: Information Research for an Urban Society, Vol. II, Papers from the Tenth Annual Conference of URISA. Claremont, CA: URISA, 1973.

Perry, J.L., and K.L. Kraemer. "Innovation attributes, policy interventions, and the diffusion of computer applications among local governments." Policy Sciences 9 (1978 April)(2): 179-205.

Pettigrew, A.M. The Politics of Organizational Decision Making. London: Tavistock, 1973.

Powers, R.F. Correlates of MIS Project Success. Minneapolis: Management Information Systems Research Center, University of Minnesota, 1971.

Public Administration Review. "Policy management assistance – A developing dialogue." Special Issue 35 (1975 December).

Public Safety Subsystem Project. "Geographic indexing support system conceptualization and system requirements." Long Beach, CA.: 1973.

Radnor, M.; A.H. Rubenstein; and D.A. Tansik. "Implementation of operations research and R&D in government and business organizations." Operations Research 18 (1970 November/December): 967-991.

Reid, W. "Interorganizational coordination: A review and critique of current theory," pp. 84-101 in P. White and B. Vlasak (eds.) Interorganizational Research in Health: Conference Proceedings. Washington, D.C.: U.S. Government Printing Office, 1972.

Reynolds, J.F. "Policy sciences: A conceptual and methodological analysis." Policy Sciences 6 (1975 March): 1-18.

Roessner, J.D. "Research and development: Making and managing policies." Policy Studies Journal 5 (1976 Winter): 205-217.

_____. "Federal policy and the application of technology to state and local government problems." Policy Analysis, in press.

Rogers, E.M. "Innovation in organizations: New research approaches." Paper presented at the Annual Meeting of American Political Science Association, San Francisco, 1975.

_____. "Effects of incentives on the diffusion of innovations: The case of family planning in Asia," pp. 133-152 in Processes and Phenomena of Social Change, ed. Gerald Zaltman. New York: Wiley, 1973.

Rogers, E.M., and R. Agarwala-Rogers. Communication in Organizations. New York: The Free Press, 1976.

Rogers, E.M., and J.D. Eveland. Innovativeness in Regional Agencies: Adoption of GBF/DIME. Ann Arbor: University of Michigan, Program in Mass Communication, 1976.

Rogers, E.M.; J.D. Eveland; and C. Klepper. The Innovation Process in Public Organizations: Some Elements of a Preliminary Model. Ann Arbor, MI: University of Michigan, Department of Journalism, 1977.

Rogers, E.M., and F.F. Shoemaker. Communications of Innovations, 2nd ed. New York: The Free Press, 1971.

Rosenbaum, W.A., and T.A. Henderson. "Explaining the attitude of community influentials toward government consolidation." Urban Affairs Quarterly 9 (1973 December): 251-275.

Schermerhorn, J.R. "Determinants of interorganizational cooperation." Academy of Management Journal 18 (1975 December): 846-856.

Schewe, C.D. "The Management information system user: An exploratory behavioral analysis." Academy of Management Journal 19 (1976 December): 577-590.

Schick, A. Budget Innovation in the States. Washington, D.C.: Brookings, 1971.

Schooler, D., Jr. "Political arenas, life styles, and the impact of technologies on policymaking." Policy Sciences 1 (1970) (2): 257-287.

Science Policy Research Unit. Project SAPPHO, A Study of Success and Failure in Innovation. Brighton, England: University of Sussex, 1971.

Siffin, W.J. "Two decades of public administration in developing countries." Public Administration Review 36 (1976 January/February): 61-71.

Staszak, J.E. "Financial management systems: Transfer for results," pp. 21-26 in Urban and Regional Information Systems: Perspectives on Information Systems, Vol. II, Papers from the Twelfth Annual Conference of URISA. Claremont, CA: URISA, 1974.

Swanson, E.B. "On Being Informed by a Computer-Based Management Information System: A Study of Involvement and Appreciation." Ph.D. dissertation, School of Business Administration, University of California, Berkeley, 1972.

Thompson, J.D. Organizations in Action. New York: McGraw-Hill, 1967.

_____. "Social interdependence, the polity, and public administration." Administration and Society 6 (1974 May): 3-24.

Thompson, V.A. "Bureaucracy and innovation." Administrative Science Quarterly 5 (1965 June): 1-20.

Turk, H. "Interorganizational networks in urban society: initial perspectives and comparative research." American Sociological Review 35 (1970 January): 1-19.

_____. "Comparative urban structure from an interorganizational perspective." Administrative Science Quarterly 18 (1973 March): 37-55.

Urban Institute. The Struggle to Bring Technology to the Cities. Washington, D.C.: The Urban Institute, 1970.

The Urbis Group. Computers, Bureaucrats and Politicians: High Technology in American Local Government. Irvine, CA: Public Policy Research Organization, in process.

USAC (Urban Information Systems Inter-Agency Committee) SUPPORT PANEL, Committee on Telecommunications, Assembly of Engineering, National Research Council. An Information Systems Resource Center for Local Governments. Washington, D.C.: National Academy of Sciences, 1976a.

_____. Local Government Information Systems - A Study of USAC and Future Applications of Computer Technology. Washington, D.C.: National Academy of Sciences, 1976 b.

Vertinsky, I., and R.T. Barth. "A model of diffusion and implementation: An exploratory study of managerial innovation, Columbia." Socio-Economic Planning Sciences 6 (1972): 153-171.

Walker, J.L. "Comment: Problems in research on the diffusion of policy innovations." American Political Science Review 67 (1973 December): 1186-1191.

_____. "The diffusion of innovations among the American states." American Political Science Review 63 (1969 September): 880-899.

Warner, K.E. "The need for some innovative concepts of innovation: An examination of research on the diffusion of innovations." Policy Sciences 5 (1974): 433-451.

Warren, R. "The concerting of decisions as a variable in organizational interaction," pp. 20-32 in M. Tuite, R. Chisholm and M. Radnor (eds.) Interorganizational Decision Making. Chicago: Aldine, 1972.

Wildavsky, A. Budgeting: A Comparative Theory of Budgetary Processes. Boston: Little, Brown, 1975.

Wilson, R. "A planned program," pp. 95-98 in Urban and Regional Information Systems: Information Research for an Urban Society, Vol. II, Papers from the Tenth Annual Conference of URISA. Claremont, CA: URISA, 1973.

Woodward, J. Industrial Organization: Behavior and Control. London: Oxford University Press, 1970.

Wynne, B.E., and G.W. Dickson. "Experienced managers' performance in experimental man-machine decision system simulation." Academy of Management Journal 18 (1975 March): 25-40.

Yin, R.; K. Heald; M. Vogel; P. Fleischauer; and B. Vladek. A Review of Case Studies of Technological Innovations in State and Local Services. Washington, D.C.: Rand, 1976.

Yin, R.K., & S.K. Quick. "Routinization I: Thinking about routinization." Santa Monica, CA: Rand, 1977. Mimeographed.

Index

Adoption
    assessment of federal policy on, 134
    definition of, 11
    influence of executive support on, 112-116, 123
    influence of staffing and organizational arrangements on, 96-102, 123
    measures of, 92, 95, 105
Adoptability, 11, 96, 80-90, 122
Agency dominance, 122, 82-84
Analytic model, of technological innovation. See Technological innovation model
Antecedents of executive support. See Determinants of executive support
Applications
    critical, 128
    design for transfer of, 66, 127
    diversity of, 5, 125, 127
    future areas of growth of, 5
    number of, 3, 5
    representative examples of, 9
    sophistication of, 5
Associated costs, 45, 50, 120-121
Automation, pattern of, 3, 5, 6

Bingham, R.D., 74, 108

Chief executive support. See Executive support

Climate favorableness, 95, 99, 100
Climate homogeneity, 95, 99
Communicability, 25, 30, 120
Communication, professional, 26, 30, 120, 133
Compatibility, technical, 56, 61, 67-68
Computing, as innovation, 2
Concept of executive support, 104
Conceptual framework, of the analyses. See Technological innovation model
Contact between executive and technology, 108, 111, 115
Cooperation, intergovernmental. See Subsystems characteristics
Correlates of executive support, 104
Costs
    associated, 41, 45, 50, 120
    relative, 25, 30
Curve fitting, adequacy of, 9-20, 37
Current utility, 104-108

Data sources, 13
Demonstration programs, 50-51
Departure from current technology, 25, 28, 31, 119-120
Design approaches, federal, 9, 131
Design for transfer, 65, 126-127
Determinants of executive support, 11, 111-116, 123-124
Development status, 95-96, 112
Diffusion of applications
    assessment of federal policy on, 125-126, 129-131

Diffusion of applications (cont'd)
    defined, 11
    distinguished from diffusion of
        computers, 2
    influence of innovation attributes
        and systems characteristics on,
        28, 119-120
    influence of subsystems char-
        acteristics on, 47-51, 120-121
    measures of, 26-27, 42
Diffusion of computers, 2
Diffusion research, 17-20, 36-37
Diversity of applications, 5, 125, 127
Documentation, 66
Downs, G.W., Jr., and L.B. Mohr,
    18, 19-20, 73, 74, 108

Evaluative capacity, local govern-
    ment, 133-134
Executive contact with technology,
    108-109, 110, 115
Executive support
    assessment of federal policy on,
        133-134
    definition of, 11
    determinants of, 111-116, 121
    influence of, 99-102, 123
    measures of, 95-96, 108
    theories about, 92, 103-105
Expected utility, 104-108
Extensiveness of transfer, 56-57
Extent of adoption, 22, 30-31, 119-
    120
External funding, 77, 82-84. See
    also Financial support, federal
Extra-organizational influences, 11.
    See also Market characteristics;
    Subsystems characteristics;
    Systems characteristics

Federal financial assistance. See
    Financial assistance, federal
Federal investment, 5
Federal policy, 2-10, 126-134
Feller, I., and D.C. Menzel, 19n, 19,
    74, 104
Financial assistance, federal
    assessment of federal policy on,
        131-132
    influence on diffusion of, 30-31,

    119-120, 129
    as measure of diffusion, 26-31
Fliegel, F., and J. Kivlin, 23

Gateway capacity, 128
Gray, V., 18n, 20

Homophily, 45, 47

Increment system building, 5-6, 127-
    128, 132-133
Innovation attributes
    defined, 10-11
    lack of attention given to in
        research, 19, 37
    influence on diffusion of, 30-31,
        119-120
    influence on transfer of, 54, 61, 63
    measure of, 22
Innovation decision research, 74
Innovation magnitude, 95, 99-100
Innovation outcomes, 11. See also
    Adoptability; Adoption; Diffusion
    of applications; Resource sharing;
    Transfer
Innovation scope, 92, 99-100
Innovations, computer applications
    as, 2
Institutional incentives for transfer,
    68-69
Integrated systems applications, 7, 9,
    67
Integration, 76-77, 80-81, 84, 87-89,
    122
Intergovernmental cooperation. See
    Subsystems characteristics
Interorganizational theory, 40-41, 50-
    51
Intra-organizational influences, 10-11.
    See also Executive support;
    Local government environment;
    Staffing and organizational arrange-
    ments
Investment, local government, 3
Investment, federal, 5

Local government environment
    conceptual frameworks of, 73-74
    defined, 11
    measures of, 76

Local gov't. environment (cont'd)
   influence on adoptability of, 80-
   90, 122-123
Local government evaluative capacity, 133-134
Local government investment, 3
Local government policy objectives,
   5-6
Locus of development, 53-54

Market characteristics, 11, 52-69,
   120, 126-127
Mechanisms for transfer, 9-10
Methodology
   for study of executive support,
   109
   for study of local government environment, 78-79
   for study of market characteristics, 56-57
   for study of staffing and organizational arrangements, 96
   for study of subsystems characteristics, 47
   for study of systems characteristics, 26-28
Models of organizational influence,
   90-91, 100-101
Mohr, L.B., 104, 108, 109

Need
   as characteristic of local government environment, 77
   influence on adoptability of, 82-
   84
   influence on diffusion and transfer of, 47
   in interorganizational theory,
   41-42
   as subsystems characteristics,
   44
Need/demand, 108-109, 111-112,
   115-116
Network arrangements. See Subsystems characteristics
Number of applications
   in development, 105
   in use, 5
Number of innovations, 73-74, 76

Opportunities to cooperate, 41-42,
   44-45, 50, 120-121
Organizational climate, 95-96, 99-100
Organizational domain, 76-77, 80, 83-
   84, 89, 122
Organizational influence, models of,
   91-92, 100-101
Origins of an innovation, 20, 37
Overhead influences on adoption, 91-
   92. See also Executive support

Past experience of transferees, 56-57
Pattern of adoption, 23, 30-31, 119-
   120
Pattern of automation, 3, 5-7
Perceived effect of user agency, 77,
   82-83, 84
Perceptual components, 104-105, 115,
   123-124
Pervasiveness, 25, 30, 31, 120
Plans for transfer, 54, 56-58
Policy, federal, 2-10, 126-133
Policy interventions, 22, 37-38, 119-
   120
Policy objectives, local government,
   5-6
Politics of innovation, 132-134
Portability of applications, 53, 64
Productivity, 1, 2
Professional communication, 26, 30,
   119-120, 133
Professionalism, 95, 103-104, 101
Proximity of transfer sites, 54, 56, 58

Radnor, M., A.H. Rubenstein, and
   D.A. Tansik, 95
Rate of adoption, 22-23, 26-27, 30-31,
   119-120
Rate of diffusion, 42, 47, 120-121
Relative cost, 25-26, 30
Reporting requirements, federal, 9-10,
   130
Research and demonstration, federal
   support of, 9-10, 130
Resistance to transfer, 68-69
Resource allocation, 96, 99-100, 101
Resource availability, 96, 99, 100
Resource sharing, 42, 50-51
Risk, 76-77, 80-81, 87-89, 122-123

Rogers, E.M., 18, 104, 108
Rogers, E.M., and R. Agarwala-Roger
    41, 108
Rogers, E.M. and J.D. Eveland, 108
Rogers, E.M., and F.F. Shoemaker,
    22-23, 25, 41, 45

Schermerhorn, J.R., 40, 69, 44
Selection bias, 18-19, 37
Selection environment, 10-11. See
    also Executive support; Local
    government environment; Market
    characteristics; Staffing and or-
    ganizational arrangements; Sub-
    systems characteristics; Systems
    characteristics
Similarity of transferees, 53-54,
    56, 57-58
Slack resources, 96, 99-100
Sophistication of applications, 5,
    54, 56, 64
Sophistication of transferees, 56,
    58, 68, 120
Specificity of evaluation, 23, 25, 30,
    31
Staff competence, 77, 82-83, 84,
    122-123
Staffing and organizational arrange-
    ments, 11, 91-102, 123
Subsidies, federal, 9-10, 131-132
Subsystems characteristics, 11, 40-
    51, 120-122
Supplier availability, 44-45, 50, 121
Supplier proximity, 77, 82-83, 84,
    122-123
Support, federal, 7, 9, 37-38, 133-
    134. See also Financial assis-
    tance, federal
Swanson, E.B., 108
Systems characteristics, 11, 17-37,
    119-120

Task complexity, 21, 24, 31, 119
Technical compatibility, 54, 56, 58,
    68
Technological innovation model, 10-
    11
    assessment of, 123-125
    executive support component
    of, 104-109

local government environment
    component of, 74-79
    market characteristics com-
    ponent of, 54
    staffing and organizational
    arrangements component of, 92-96
    subsystems characteristics com-
    ponent of, 42-45
    systems characteristics component
    of, 20-27

Technological performance, 109-112,
    115
Trade-off inducements, 45, 47
Transfer
    assessment of federal policy toward,
    133
    characteristics of, 56-57, 127-128
    common beliefs about, 52
    influence of market characteristics
    on, 56-69, 126-127
    influence of subsystems character-
    istics on, 50
    measures of, 42, 54
Transfer mechanisms, federal, 9-10,
    131
Turk, H., 42, 44

Uncertainty, 77, 83, 84
Urban Information Systems Inter-
    Agency Committee (USAC), 9
User involvement, 96, 98-100
Utility
    current, 104-108
    expected, 104-108

Visibility of innovation, 77, 80-82, 84,
    122-123

Warner, K.E., 17, 18, 19
Warren, R., 76

Yin, et al., 74, 108

About the Authors

JAMES L. PERRY is an Assistant Professor of Administration in the Graduate School of Administration, University of California, Irvine. He received his M.P.A. and Ph.D. from the Maxwell School of citizenship and Public Affairs, Syracuse University. Dr. Perry has authored and co-authored numerous articles.

KENNETH L. KRAEMER is Director of the Public Policy Research Organization and Associate Professor in the Graduate School of Administration of the University of California, Irvine. Dr. Kraemer received his M.P.A. and Ph.D. from the University of Southern California. He has been a consultant to the federal Urban Information Systems Inter-Agency Committee (USAC) and is principle investigator for the URBIS (Urban Information Systems) project. The author of Policy Analysis in Local Government, Dr. Kraemer is also the co-author of several books and has published monographs, as well as numerous articles in both academic and practitioner journals.

Pergamon Policy Studies

No. 1   Laszlo—*The Objectives of the New International Economic Order*

No. 2   Link/Feld—*The New Nationalism*

No. 3   Ways—*The Future of Business*

No. 4   Davis—*Managing and Organizing Multinational Corporations*

No. 5   Volgyes—*The Peasantry of Eastern Europe, Volume One*

No. 6   Volgyes—*The Peasantry of Eastern Europe, Volume Two*

No. 7   Hahn/Pfaltzgraff—*The Atlantic Community in Crisis*

No. 8   Renninger—*Multinational Cooperation for Development in West Africa*

No. 9   Stepanek—*Bangledesh—Equitable Growth?*

No. 10 Foreign Affairs—*America and the World 1978*

No. 11 Goodman/Love—*Management of Development Projects*

No. 12 Weinstein—*Bureacratic Opposition*

No. 13 De Volpi—*Proliferation, Plutonium, and Policy*

No. 14 Francisco/Laird/Laird—*The Political Economy of Collectivized Agriculture*

No. 15 Godet—*The Crisis in Forecasting and the Emergence of the "Prospective" Approach*

No. 16 Golany—*Arid Zone Settlement Planning*

No. 17 Perry/Kraemer—*Technological Innovation in American Local Governments*

No. 18 Carman—*Obstacles to Mineral Development*

No. 19 Demir—*Arab Development Funds in the Middle East*

No. 20 Kahan/Ruble—*Industrial Labor in the U.S.S.R.*

No. 21 Meagher—*An International Redistribution of Wealth and Power*

No. 22 Thomas/Wionczek—*Integration of Science and Technology With Development*

No. 23 Mushkin/Dunlop—*Health: What Is It Worth?*

No. 24 Abouchar—*Economic Evaluation of Soviet Socialism*

No. 25 Amos—*Arab-Israeli Military/Political Relations*

No. 26 Geismar/Geismar—*Families in an Urban Mold*

No. 27 Leitenberg/Sheffer—*Great Power Intervention in the Middle East*

No. 28 O'Brien/Marcus—*Crime and Justice in America*

No. 29 Gartner—*Consumer Education in the Human Services*

No. 30 Diwan/Livingston—*Alternative Development Strategies and Appropriate Technology*

No. 31 Freedman—*World Politics and the Arab-Israeli Conflict*

No. 32 Williams/Deese—*Nuclear Nonproliferatrion*

No. 33 Close—*Europe Without Defense?*

No. 34 Brown—*Disaster Preparedness*

No. 35 Grieves—*Transnationalism in Politics and Business*